MW01289756

Escaping The Evil Clown: The Alcohol Illusion
Extended Edition:

By Craig Beck

Published by Craig Beck Media Limited 2017

www.craigbeck.com

www.StopDrinkingExpert.com

Escaping The Evil Clown

By Craig Beck

Copyright Craig Beck Media Limited

Hypnosis reprogramming tracks mentioned in this book are available to download from

www.stopdrinkingexpert.com

This book is for my children - Jordan & Aoife… always my inspiration to be a better human being.

Alcohol is a drug that has achieved the ultimate illusion. It has managed to convince everyone in the western world that it isn't a drug at all, but rather a harmless social pleasantry.

A product that does none of the things that the marketing promises and yet remains unchallenged by society and continues to be endorsed by the government.

Alcohol is a substance that kills over 2,500,000 people a year and yet still remains legal in virtually every country around the world.

Craig Beck is known as the Stop Drinking Expert because he helps people to see the truth about alcohol. The shocking reality that is hidden behind the smoke and mirrors of the marketing and our own self created social conditioning.

His book Alcohol Lied to Me has topped bestseller charts for many years and has been translated into several different languages.

"Alcohol is the ultimate wolf in sheep's clothing, a deeply insidious and dangerous drug packaged into pretty bottles and marketed as a fun, social pleasantry by the drinks manufacturers. The western world is conditioned from birth to believe that good times and alcohol go hand in hand.

In reality consuming this drug is like playing a very dangerous game of Buckaroo, the longer you keep playing the more chance you have the mule will kick and destroy your world", Craig Beck

In this specially extended edition of his Alcohol Illusion series, Craig explains how you are not your addiction. You are not weak willed or broken. Alcoholism affects millions of people regardless of their gender, location, intelligence or social standing.

Craig helps to explain this by describing your addiction to alcohol as though it is an Evil Clown that lives inside your head. Whispering encouragement in your ear as though he is your best friend. However, the smile is only painted on and this clown is actually your worst enemy.

Using the techniques in this book you can effectively and easily create separation between the real you and the addicted version of you. This is powerful because the moment you can see how the Evil Clown is pulling your strings, is the same moment you slip out of his grasp.

All magic loses its power when you discover how the trick is done and the same is true of the alcohol trap. Knowledge is power and this book will help you to easily stop drinking without ineffective willpower, dangerous medication or expensive rehab.

About The Author

I didn't realize it at the time but my childhood was heavily tainted by alcohol from a very early age. I am in no doubt that it played a part in me eventually developing a problem with it.

During my twenties I kept up with my friends in the drinking stakes. I was very sociable and would be the first to agree to a night in the pub. I drank faster and more than anyone else I knew – they considered me to be the life and soul of the party… a man who could handle his drink! I was proud of this reputation and at this point in my life, it didn't worry me in the slightest.

Alcohol was not dominating my thinking; I was just the same as any other young man – drinking to have a good time.

> "I didn't want to stop drinking, I had a reputation for being a big man who could handle my drink"

I am not sure at what point my drinking habit changed from 'social pleasantry' to being the primary focus of my day-to-day life. Such is the deceptive nature of this drug, it takes so long to get hooked that you don't even notice there is a problem (until it is too late). It is very much like the timeworn story of the frog in the boiling pan of water. If you drop a live frog into a boiling pan of water it will jump straight out in shock, but if you place the frog in cold water and slowly increase the heat it will eventually boil to death – this is alcohol addiction personified.

In my early thirties I started to question if my drinking was normal, of course deep down inside I knew it wasn't but I was desperate to prove to myself that I wasn't doing anything wrong. I probably spent five years fighting to keep drinking; I just couldn't see how life could be worth living without alcohol.

I was so out of control I refused to go anywhere with my friends or family that prevented me from drinking. Even if I went to the movies I would sneak a bottle of whiskey into the theatre with me so I could add it so the Coca-Cola I was going to sip all the way through the film.

Alcohol turned me into a bad father and a bad husband. I would refuse to go anywhere with the family unless I could be sure I could drink once I got there.

Eventually my drinking started to affect my health and at this point I started to sit up and take notice that what I was doing wasn't normal. I became very scared about what was happening and I tried everything I could to wrestle control back from the drug.

I tried locking away my alcohol and giving the key to my wife, I tried going cold turkey, forcing myself to have painful dry months and I even bought dangerous prescription only medication online. Absolutely nothing made the slightest bit of difference to my drinking.

Eventually I reached rock bottom… I was at my lowest point, I had tried everything and yet I was drinking more than I ever had in my life. I was slowly killing myself and I simply couldn't slow down. It was at that point that I decided I had to do something different or I was going to die and leave my children without a father.

I needed a paradigm shift of massive proportions; I had to see the situation from the outside looking in. I leant on my former training as a human behavior expert and clinical hypnotist and I started to see a pattern or a loop in what I was doing.

Once I identified the triggers that started me drinking and encouraged me to keep repeating the process it was as though a light bulb flickered into life in my mind. It was a eureka moment where it suddenly became so clear to me that I hadn't previously been able to stop drinking because I believed that alcohol was a benefit that I would be deprived of if I chose a life of abstinence.

I realized that as long as I believed alcohol to be a positive object in my life there would be no way to give it up. So instead of treating the symptoms of alcohol addiction I started to address the root cause of it; my erroneous beliefs.

One day, I picked up a bottle of very expensive French wine and I placed it on the desk in my office. I sat staring at it for over an hour and a thought popped into my head: 'attractively packaged poison'.

That's all it is, I thought. It doesn't matter whether it is priceless French Bordeaux or cheap cider; the component part of the drink is always the same. All these designer alcohol brands are nothing more than poison hidden in a pretty bottle and marketed with billions of euros to make us believe they are a benefit.

Alcohol is not a treat, a way to celebrate or a social pleasantry. It is nothing more than 'attractively packaged poison'. Once you get to the point where you can see the truth the rest of the journey becomes easy.

How can consuming a poison be any sort of benefit? The answer of course is it can't – the problem is most of the western world is trapped in the delusion that if you remove the thing that is causing them misery and pain their life will somehow get worse. Once you are outside looking in you can see the madness for what it truly is… madness!

The Evil Clown

"A lot of people think that addiction is a choice. A lot of people think it's a matter of will. That has not been my experience. I don't find it to have anything to do with strength", Matthew Perry

My name is Craig Beck and I am an ex problem drinker… that statement almost certainly causes a picture to automatically form in your minds eye as to what I looked like back then.

However, the chances are good that the picture you see is a long way from the reality, because just like you I was not a stereotypical drunk. I was never found stumbling around the streets or sat looking disheveled on the local park bench. Neither am I one of those big Hollywood stars who proudly announce (via their agent) that they are back in rehab again. I was your average Joe, a family man with a decent career who managed to hide his two bottles of wine a night drink habit for well over a decade.

That actually makes me sound much more deceitful than I actually am. In reality for a large period of that time I honestly believed I had no reason to hide my drinking habits because I was doing nothing out of the ordinary.

When I eventually did start to question what I was doing, rather than change my behavior I simply made sure I was surrounded by people who used alcohol to the same extent that I did. I did this purely to validate my actions and prove to myself that I was normal, granting myself a license to continue my affair with the drug I loved.

I was what they call a 'functioning alcoholic', I drank to excess every day but the next morning you wouldn't have had a clue I had had anything more than a sniff of the barmaid's apron. I was successful in my career, a director of several companies and even the trustee of a large children's charity. This 'normal' lifestyle represents the vast majority of people dealing with alcohol addiction. The drunk 'down and out' swigging back cheap booze in the park is just the stereotype other drinkers have created as if to provide visible proof that they are not similarly afflicted.

I battled my drink habit for longer than I care to remember. I swung violently from denial to despair as I wrestled with this substance that I hated and loved with equal measure. My whole life became about planning my next drink and then dealing with the crushing guilt I always felt afterwards. This pain would force me to come up with more and more complicated ways to try and trick myself to stop drinking.

Eventually after many years of failed attempts to retake control I cracked it. I had a "eureka" moment which let me see alcohol in a completely different light. Only when I stopped seeing it as a benefit and realized that it makes every aspect of life worse did I stop wanting to drink.

This drug very nearly destroyed my life and I am eternally grateful to be a long time free of its cycle of destruction. I now teach other people how to also get free from alcohol via my online rehab site www.StopDrinkingExpert.com and via my other books on the subject.

Alcohol rewires your brain to ensure you keep using the drug. It achieves this over such a long period of time that you are completely unaware of it doing so. So when you stop drinking it takes an equally long time for your brain to start thinking like a sober person again. It is a very slow process of reawakening to life without a devious and dangerous drug continuously sloshing around in your body.

Over the last five sober years of my life I have had a lot of time to reflect on how alcohol affected my behavior over the decades that I was a slave to it. My rose tinted glasses have long since been discarded and I can now observe other drinkers with more clarity and prospective than ever before. I might be free of it personally but I am still forced to watch people I love continue to drink, still trapped in the cycle. I now witness firsthand the denial and delusion proffered forth by all drinkers of this insidious drug. The same bullshit and illogical nonsense that I also used to preach at anyone who dared to question my drinking.

I describe alcohol as devious because of the slow but powerful way it traps the drinker into the loop of addiction. The first time you tasted alcohol was most likely the same way that I did… sneaking a sip of your father's booze when he asked you to be a good boy or girl and bring him a glass of it. I remember it like it was yesterday, I was eight years old and we had moved into our new home. It was so spacious and luxurious compared to the horrible apartment above a butcher's shop that we had squeezed ourselves into while the building work got underway on what would be our family home for the rest of my childhood years.

All the furniture was brand new and my parents still insisted on leaving the plastic sheeting on everything to preserve the newness for as long as possible. The air was thick with the strong but not unpleasant smell of the new carpets. My parents both came from humble 'working class' backgrounds and this house represented something very significant to them. It had stretched them to the limit financially and at times it seemed as though they had bitten off much more than they could chew. But yet, here they were at the end of the journey in their glorious new home. Bigger and more splendid than anything anyone on either side of the family had ever managed to achieve.

You could sense the pride oozing from my dad as he quite literally sat in his new throne, the king of his castle. He surveyed his kingdom and was happy. Such a moment in life should be savored and cherished which he did as he called out for his eldest son and I came running.

"Be a good lad and get your dad a whiskey from the new drinks cabinet in the dining room", he said with huge grin.

Having spent the last six months all squeezed into a tiny one bedroom flat you could tell the fact that we even had another room was such a novelty and a thrill for us all. Never mind that we had a dining room, a room just to eat in – wow the opulence of it all.

I ran to my mother and asked her for a whiskey glass. She opened a velvet-lined box, like something that you would expect to contain precious jewels. Opening it she passed me a glass so new that it still had a sticker on the side. It was so much heavier than it looked and I was quickly warned to be careful with it because it was 'Crystal', whatever that meant, certainly nothing significant to my eight year old self! But the warning in itself said that this was not just a guy having a drink this was some sort of very special ritual and both parents were acting like it was a big deal.

I remember thinking when I drink my milk I don't have a special glass so what is so special about 'this whiskey' that it needs to be contained in something this extraordinary?

I carried the glass like it was a precious newborn baby bird resting in the palm of my hands. I walked into the dining room and flicked the light switch on, the new chandelier instantly filled the new decorated room with a warm light and I walked over to the drinks cabinet. The whiskey was already on top in a decanter equally as elegant as the glass I had waiting to pour it into. Also made of thick, expensive crystal with a giant glass stopper it was almost too heavy to lift, but I managed. Splashing uneven shots of whiskey into the glass until it was about a third full.

This was every small child's biggest challenge, not only to have the responsibility of carrying something so expensive but then to fill it with liquid too – I was running the gauntlet. This was perhaps the most important moment I had ever felt in my life, such pressure but oh what an honor. I remember feeling smug that there would be no way my younger brother Mark would be entrusted with such a task, he was a notorious spiller – this was way beyond him, a man's job if ever there was one.

Walking even more slowly and delicately than before with the heavy glass now containing this strong smelling but apparently magical liquid. I made it to the middle of the room before curiosity got the better of me; I nervously lifted the glass to my mouth. The first sensation to hit me was the smell, it was disgusting! It reminded me of the thick, black creosote that the groundskeeper at school used to mark out the football field with. Obviously, I then assumed the pleasure must come from the taste and not the aroma, for how could it… it was vile smelling stuff. Ignoring the smell and trusting in the hype I proceeded to take a large gulp of the golden water and waited for the magic to happen.

There was no magic… only fire! The burning liquid rushed through my young mouth and the most horrid medicine I had ever tasted assaulted my senses like a firework exploding in my mouth. The burning horribleness spread everywhere in milliseconds and quickly hit the back of my throat. I coughed and spluttered the liquid all over the new dining table and onto the brand new cream carpet. I gasped and held back the urge to cry but I had made enough noise to send my mother running from the kitchen. I was traumatized by the awful liquid but I also knew I was in big trouble because the firewater was strictly for grown ups. If they found out I had tried it I would be grounded for a month.

With less than a second to spare I tipped the full glass of whiskey over myself, soaking my PJ's in the disgusting smelly liquid and started to cry, half to add credibility to my story and half because I really wanted to cry.

When my mum burst into the room I sobbed that I had tripped and spilt my father's whiskey. Once she realized I was not hurt her attention turned to her new carpet and I was ordered off to bed as she furiously dabbed at the liquor stains which now were speckled across the new floor.

I tugged off my wet PJ's and threw them in the wash and lay on my bed wondering why on earth grown-ups could enjoy that horrible stuff so much?

I wondered… How can people get addicted to something that tastes so bad?

This is the first layer of false protection that people believe they have against developing a problem with alcohol. Even children who grow up in alcoholic homes can taste the stuff and confidently declare 'I will never get hooked to alcohol like my Dad (or Mom) because it tastes horrible'. What they can't account for at this early stage is the power of alcohol to rewire your brain to believe all manner of crazy things that don't make the slightest bit of sense to the sober mind.

So what happens to the taste of alcohol over time? Do you think in the ten or twenty years since you had your first drink the manufacturers have found a way to make it taste better? Of course not... Alcohol tastes disgusting, it always has and it always will. If you currently believe that you genuinely enjoy the taste of it then you should see this as evidence that the rewiring is complete and it has you trapped in the illusion. To people like me you are standing in front of me chewing on an onion and claiming it's the best apple you ever tasted.

The taste of alcohol has never changed – only your perception of it changes. The drug performs this illusion so slowly that I can't help be in awe at how well it achieves its first goal. Nobody develops a problem overnight; actually the usual time period is closer to a decade than it is to a day. Such problems that develop so slowly embed themselves exceptionally deep in the subconscious mind.

Like a computer virus that hides its destructive payload in the boot sector of a disc alcohol hides its code in the parts of your mind that you are prevented from accessing. Given free reign our conscious mind would be like a small child left to wonder unsupervised in a fine china store. Do you really want the ability to tamper with the program that controls your body temperature or how often your heart beats? We would all be dead within minutes! In this secure area of the mind; alcohol uses the power of the human brain to create physical pathways to complete the drinking subroutine. If you are a regular drinker there is actual tissue in your brain designed to facilitate the habit. This is why demanding that somebody stops drinking or taking the 'just pull yourself together' approach with a drinker won't make a bit of difference. It would be like me ordering you to never move your index finger again… or else!

Alcohol has slowly turned you into a machine that runs on booze. If you have spent a decade or more living with alcohol then the drug will have already created hundreds of physical pathways in your mind. This new meat in your head is going to leave you believing all sorts of nonsense to keep the drug active. So convincing is this mental rewiring that you won't only believe the lies but you will also preach them on behalf of the drug.

You will proudly tell people that red wine is good for your heart and that's why you drink it, you will declare that a party must have alcohol to be worth attending, you will subscribe to the policy that celebrations must be accompanied by expensive fizzy wine from France, white wine makes fish taste better, a steak is incomplete without a deep red and you will continue to stroke the sheep blissfully unaware of the wolf that lies beneath the fleece.

Only after several years of being free of this drug have I been able to see how it works, and the more I see the more I despise it. In my book "Alcohol Lied to me' I make the grand claim that I am entirely comfortable around other drinkers.

This, I now realize is only partly true and while being in the company of alcohol never makes me want to drink it, in the same way I can open a tube of glue without wanting to stuff it up my nose - I see equal benefit to both drugs. I am increasingly uncomfortable watching my friends, family and loved ones using alcohol.

When I watch my mum drinking wine or my partner 'relaxing' in front of the television with a 'nice glass of red' I see what they cannot. The evil puppet master above their head with a twisted smile on his face, using his invisible string and ventriloquism to awkwardly control the person below. I hear the same brainwashed statements coming from all drinkers regardless of color, creed or sex. Challenges to the drug nearly always result in angry and offended pronouncements such as:

'What I am doing is normal, everyone drinks!'
'I can stop anytime I want'
'I am in total control; I will never have a problem'
'How dare you suggest I have a problem?'

Drinkers get angry and upset when you challenge their drinking and they see this response as normal. Would they get so upset if I questioned their use of mayonnaise? I doubt it! Defending the drug is a clear sign that the virus has been implanted... you are addicted!

I can't tell you how distressing I find it to hear people I love get angry with me because I dared to attack the drug they subscribe to. They are completely unaware of their motivation to attack and how illogical their emotional response to what I have said actually is. From my side of the argument, I can only describe it as being trapped in a dark room with someone you love.

Thankfully I have a pair of night vision glasses on and I am able to advise them of the danger that I can see lurking in the darkness. Despite the fact that they are completely blind they still insist that they know better, offended at the very suggestion that I can see anything at all. On they continue regardless of what I know is coming, and what I am desperately trying to warn them about.

Alcohol is a very clever and malicious magician. Today we think of magic as the stage shows of David Blaine, Dynamo and David Copperfield, it is generally thought to be a bit of harmless fun (but then so is alcohol). Magic has always had half a foot in the dark side of life due to the essential elements of deceit and deception that make the skill possible. It has been used for thousands of years to entertain but also distract attention while a crime is committed. Slight of hand is about forcing your prospect to focus on something insignificant while they ignore another much more important maneuver happening out of sight.

Alcohol is a evil clown; it wows you, entertains you and performs illusions for you. It makes ugly people handsome and boring people funny; trick after trick it performs for an audience always crying for more. But the smiling happy face is only painted on. Underneath the greasepaint there is a twisted, snarling mouth full of razor sharp teeth.

The evil clown is distracting your attention while he is busy stealing what is most important to you. An exceptionally adept piece of slight of hand, executed perfectly and way beyond the capabilities of any other circus illusionist living or dead.

Alcohol uses this dark illusion to cover its tracks. It is a silent thief and it is more ruthless than any human version you will ever meet. Alcohol the magical and yet sinister puppet master who will make you dance while he is busy stealing your time, health, money, relationships, intelligence, career and eventually your life. As a short sighted parasite will continue to gorge on its host until it eventually takes so much that it kills it. Alcohol will not stop until you have nothing more to give – everything is fair game and he is relentless.

Magicians never reveal their secrets because as soon as you know how they do it… they no longer have the ability to fool you. Alcohol is an addictive drug, it doesn't want you to know how it hooks you in and it doesn't want you to be aware of what it does while you are looking the other way. This book is your personal pair of night vision goggles into the dark world of alcohol 'our favourite social drug'.

Are you ready to see how the evil clown performs the trick?

"I mean, that's at least in part why I ingested chemical waste - it was a kind of desire to abbreviate myself. To present the CliffNotes of the emotional me, as opposed to the twelve-column read.

I used to refer to my drug use as putting the monster in the box. I wanted to be less, so I took more - simple as that. Anyway, I eventually decided that the reason Dr. Stone had told me I was hypomanic was that he wanted to put me on medication instead of actually treating me. So I did the only rational thing I could do in the face of such as insult - I stopped talking to Stone, flew back to New York, and married Paul Simon a week later." – Carrie Fisher

It may seem slightly schizophrenic to suggest that you and your addiction are two separate things. However, in my many years of dealing with alcohol addicted individuals I have never once concluded that the person in question is 'broken', 'weak' or 'just plain stupid'.

In actual fact I have noticed that alcohol seems to pray particularly on the intelligent and introverted more than most. Brainpower, creative thinking and introversion are all a curse as much as they are a gift. If an individual manages to harness and focus this state of mind they can achieve truly breathtaking things. However, if left without boundaries and direction it can make a person beyond miserable.

Uncontrolled introversion can lead to chronic overthinking, depression, worry, anxiety and panic. When someone like this discovers alcohol the Evil Clown really sits up and pays attention. The clown knows that these people need to be nurtured and cared for because they are easy to hook into the drug.

Alcohol gives us over thinkers a tool to stop the craziness of our minds for a brief moment. If alcohol wasn't hell bent on destroying every aspect of our lives, some might be able to claim it's a worthwhile tool. However, that's a bit like saying rain would be great if it didn't get you wet. The Evil Clown wants these people dead and he will stop at nothing until he gets this result.

At the moment it probably doesn't make a great deal of sense that there is a third party living inside you. But let me explain how I know this to be true.

When you develop a drink problem you are acutely aware of just how much damage is being done to your life. Everything that ever mattered to you is under violent attack. Your finances are crashing, your relationships are dying, your career is treading water (at best) and your health is starting to fail. Yet, despite everything falling down around you, there is still a voice in your head that says 'what you need to deal with this is a drink'.

This is quite clearly an insane viewpoint. It would be like going to hospital with cancer and the doctor suggesting they are going to try and cure the problem by giving you more cancer. However, nobody I ever met in my member's area is clinically insane. So where does this unhinged view come from?

The Evil Clown

99.9% of your brain is beautiful, powerful and capable of creating amazing things in your life. However, buried deep in the middle is the Evil Clown. He is small but noisy. Let me prove that he is there:

Stop reading for a moment and sit quietly for a few moments. Next I want you to vividly imagine never being allowed to have another alcoholic drink again for the rest of your life.

Most drinkers will feel a sensation of panic, fear and denial. They feel all these counter intuitive sensations despite how desperate they are to quit drinking. This insane noise is the Clown screaming in horror.

He doesn't' usually lose his cool like that. The Evil Clown is clever; he can generally control his temper. He can for the most part keep the smile painted on his face and whisper nicely in your ear. He is a master manipulator and like all control freaks he will do what it takes to get the outcome he wants.

My daughter is a ninja of this sort of persuasion technology. If she wants something she doesn't just ask for it (like my son would do). She will tell me how much she loves me, how much of a great Dad I am and how lucky she feels to have me in her life… then and only then she will drop the bomb. "Dad, you know how my sneakers are looking a little old now. Would you mind buying me some more at the Mall today?'

When you get home after a hard day at work, the Evil Clown wants you straight onto the drug. Alcohol gives him power and control. However, despite how much he wants to, he doesn't just scream 'drink alcohol you asshole' in your ear. Instead he acts like my daughter does when she wants some new sneakers. He gently whispers in your inner ear. He tells you how great you are that you got through such a tough day. He tells you that you deserve to let off some steam and really kick back. Have a drink and relax my friend, it's about time you did something for yourself.

He doesn't need to keep this performance up for long, he knows the moment you take the first sip he has you. The drug will do the rest, he can go back to bed and leave you to it.

Have you noticed that you sometimes let out a beautifully deep outward sigh when you take your first drink of the day? But you never do it with the second drink. This is the Evil Clown screaming in ecstasy that yet again he tricked you, and so easily too.

At first this concept may feel scary but there is some very good news. The Clown can't survive unless you feed him. He has no way of nourishing himself and unless you provide for him he will quickly lose power and eventually fall into a deep coma. You will notice I didn't say die! The Evil Clown can never die. One glass of alcohol at anytime will act like a heart defibrillator, violently slamming him back into the waking world.

No, you can't kill him but you can easily sentence him to a lifetime in a tiny prison cell. And for the sort of crimes this twisted malevolent demon has committed there can be no more fitting place for him to rot away his time.

The Stop Drinking Expert program has a secret Facebook group. Today I saw this amazing post and I wanted to share it with you.

Some personal names, locations and details have been changed to protect the anonymity of the member but the rest remains as was written.

Hi everyone,

I have some free time and I am a little bored so I thought I would check in!

Some of you probably know already that I work away from home most weeks, usually 3 to 4 nights (I am a salesman) and now and again maybe 5, I have done this for years.

For years I lived in hotels, usually a different one every night. I got fed up with the whole thing, packing and unpacking every day, checking in and checking out and being on your own in a hotel bar every night was no fun.

I honestly believe this was the start of my drinking every day... I piled on weight not only through the alcohol consumption but also the poor food choices I would make.

My bar bills where huge most nights paying hotel prices. Often I would pay for them out of my own cash rather than the company credit card to hide it from my wife.

I fell into a habit of drinking early and quickly in the knowledge that if I got to bed early I would be able to function (just about) the day after.

I started to dislike my job spending every day feeling jaded and being impatient with the clients I was trying to sell to.

The First Sober Year

When I did my first almost year AF I found it even more tedious, this was nothing to do with me wanting a drink or being tempted I just found it boring.

Being sober I noticed more and more that the menu choices for someone trying to eat healthy was basically a salad and nothing else.

So I decided enough was enough and I bought myself a motor home and I now travel the UK and sometimes beyond, working away in my own little home from home.

Its fantastic and although I miss my family terribly when I am away. It is still much better than hotel living.

I see more of the outdoors, I cook for myself and have it stocked with everything I need in terms of food, drink and supplements. I have TV, DVD's and even a WiFi ariel on the roof for internet!

The extra time we have on our hands is a wonderful thing, but it can lead to a feeling of boredom. So be ready for that and plan new fun stuff to add into your life.

We need to be grateful for this extra time; our time here on this planet is short enough without wasting it in a drunken fog.

Time is Valuable

There are so many people are terminally ill with just days left to live, who would no doubt give anything for a few extra days.

It's crazy that us newly sober folk complain about time on our hands. I for one am not going to be negative about all this extra time, stopping drinking a poison has given me.

When you are free from the alcohol trap and the haze lifts there are aspects in your life that need to be addressed and changes that need to be made. This is a good thing… trust me on that!

At least being sober now we are dealing with the issue head on and not hiding behind a drug.

Saddens me to think that for years my one and only hobby was drinking a poisonous drug… when you stop that pastime you have so much more time for others.

I am typing this from my Motor home on a campsite in Scotland.

I was working yesterday and I am working here tomorrow and as it is a 6 hour return drive home and back it was pointless me going home. So it has left me with a free day!

Its pouring down outside and I am finding the noise of rain on the roof quite relaxing.

The other great thing about being sober is…
All my work is complete!

My inbox is empty because I am top of everything. Just before starting on this post I had everything done, a clear desk so to speak!

Its lunchtime here now, and I have found out that there is a theme park just down the road.

So as soon as this rain stops I am going to the theme park and spending the rest of the day being a big kid and riding fairground rides!

Sorry for the long rambling post, some of you may find it useful. I know I enjoyed writing it. Being sober is wonderful, I am so grateful.

Sober & Proud

David

"Though no one can go back and make a brand new start, anyone can start from now and make a brand new ending." – Carl Bard

'Time me, gentlemen!'

It's just after midday on a late spring day in 1842 and the wooden viewing galleries that surround the operating room of University College Hospital, London, are packed.

Sir Robert Liston, the foremost surgeon of his age, and a man whose temper is as sharp as his chiseled features, is about to begin work.

The assembled crowds of anxious medical students dutifully check their pocket watches, as two of Liston's surgical assistants - 'dressers' as they are called - take firm hold of the struggling patient's shoulders.

The fully conscious man, already racked with pain from the badly broken leg he suffered by falling between a train and the platform at nearby King's Cross station, looks in total horror at the collection of knives, saws and needles that lie alongside him.

Liston clamps his left hand across the patient's thigh, picks up his favorite knife and in one rapid movement makes his incision. A dresser immediately tightens a tourniquet to stem the blood.

As the patient screams with pain, Liston puts the knife away and grabs the saw. With an assistant exposing the bone, Liston begins to cut.

Suddenly, the nervous student who has been volunteered to steady the injured leg realizes he is supporting its full weight. With a shudder he drops the severed limb into a waiting box of sawdust.

Liston, however, is still busy, tying off the main artery of the thigh with a reef knot and then tying off other smaller blood vessels, at one point even holding the thread in his mouth. As the tourniquet is loosened, the flesh is stitched.

It is hard to imagine today but there really was a time where this gruesome style of surgery was commonplace, a time before general anaesthetic. When the strongest stuff the surgeon could offer you was a swig from his trusty hip flask before he began to cut into your acutely conscious body.

As usual when I start writing a new book the planets do tend to align, creating spooky real life examples to help me emphasize the point I am trying to make. I started writing my weight loss book, Fat Guy Friday on a flight from Cyprus to the United Kingdom. No sooner had I started typing did two giant 300 lbs. guys come and announce they had the two seats either side of me. I spent the entire five-hour flight squashed between their wobbly guts, which overhung the armrests by at least a foot on either side. I won't lie to you, while I appreciated the irony of the situation I was desperate to get off that aircraft. Firstly because of the discomfort of travelling like a veal calf but secondly, and most significantly, because the two gentlemen providing my padded enclosure had read every word I had written and no doubt thought it was some sort of personal agenda against them. I don't blame them and I did slightly fear for my safety as I named them Shrek One and Shrek Two in the book. I have never typed as fast in my life, desperate to get that section of the manuscript up above the fold of the screen before they joined forces to squash me like a Panini between the hot plates.

As I introduce you to the anesthetic nature of alcohol, I find myself writing this section of Escaping The Evil Clown from my sick bed having just endured an operation of my own. A slight genetic defect had caused my hip socket to overdevelop during childhood and the years of wear and tear since then have caused a rip to appear in the labrum around the joint. Until fairly recently this was an untreatable condition that would eventually lead to a full hip replacement. Thankfully advances in medical science and specifically keyhole surgery mean that the tear can now be repaired and the offending overgrowth of bone filed down to prevent further damage to the hip.

The operation is called a hip arthroscopy, which involves the leg being stretched until the hip dislocates. This is achieved with a contraption that looks quite similar to a medieval torture device, which was known as 'The Rack'. I knew far too much about the operation I was about to have thanks in part to YouTube and my over inquisitive mind. As a result I have discovered that information is not always power and often it's much better to remain completely uninformed, head in the sand ostrich style. As they say; you can't un-see things no matter how much you want to and there is no doubt this unnecessary curiosity helped turn me into an embarrassing, gibbering wreck on the day of my admission to Harrogate Hospital in North Yorkshire.

Thanks to a spinal block and general anesthetic I felt none of the torture my body was to be put through. A double whammy of pain preventing measures to ensure I neither felt anything during the operation itself or for eight to nine hours directly after it. Despite such comprehensive medical care I am afraid to stay it did not prevent me acting like a complete big girl's blouse when I sat in the anaesthetic room awaiting an epidural that would render me paralyzed from the waist down. A very desirable state to be in considering 'The Rack' was waiting on the other side of the swing doors at the opposite end of the room.

The nurses tried to calm me by asking questions about my day-to-day life. Trying to slow my panicky heart rate down by asking what I thought of the local football team's performance at the weekend. Ashen faced I tried my best to join in the distracting small talk but I was genuinely terrified about what was coming next. I can't imagine how I would have coped in those times before modern day medical procedures and drugs… oh the drugs, God bless those drugs!

If alcohol is a harmless bit of fun, why did naval doctors and Victorian surgeons reach for the rum and not something else?

The answer is Alcohol is not a harmless inert substance. Alcohol is indeed a mild anaesthetic, a chemical that interferes with our brain chemistry until it cannot function as it was designed to. Of course when you are having your leg amputated you really need something a long way from 'mild' to take the edge off the procedure but it was all they had and so it was welcomed all the same.

Difficulty walking, blurred vision, slurred speech, slowed reaction times, impaired memory: all side effects of the drug we collectively declare to be nothing more than a social pleasantry.

Some of these impairments are detectable after only one or two drinks and quickly resolve when drinking stops. On the other hand, a person who drinks heavily over a long period of time may have brain deficits that persist well after he or she achieves sobriety.

Imagine if a chocolate bar was released to market today and shortly after it went on general sale it was found to have anaesthetic properties and if within days consumers were crashing their cars into each other, being admitted to hospital with an array of serious and sometimes fatal side effects. How long do you think this product would remain on the shelves? It would be banned in no time at all and the company behind it would be so comprehensively sued that they would surely go bust in a hurry.

Alcohol does all this and more, yet it remains on supermarket shelves around the world with a licence to be marketed as literally anything the drinking manufacturer desires. No other product has such freedom; alcohol can be portrayed as fun, sexy, aspirational and can even promise to make people like you more!

Imagine if a tyre company ran a TV commercial that claimed fitting your automobile with their new winter cross ply will make you more attractive to the opposite sex and lead to more success at work! This would be labelled as false advertising and deemed misleading to the general public! The commercials would probably never see the light of day and yet alcohol makes a never-ending array of erroneous promises that go unchallenged.

Exactly how alcohol affects the brain and the likelihood of reversing the impact of heavy drinking remain hot topics in alcohol research today. We do know that heavy drinking may have extensive and far–reaching effects on the brain, ranging from simple "slips" in memory to permanent and debilitating conditions that require lifetime custodial care. And even moderate drinking leads to short–term impairment, as shown by extensive research on the impact of drinking on driving.

This killer product escapes virtually all our current regulations and safeguards because it has been around long enough to set its own precedent. The fact that 'everyone drinks' and our parents, grandfparents and generations as far back as we can recall also drank alcohol, makes us incorrectly believe we are protected by the assumed safety in numbers principle. Actually that is not true, no drinker really believes that he or she is protected because of the social proof around the drug, he or she is just pleased to have another weapon in his or her arsenal to justify their behaviour around a substance that we all inherently know is dangerous and unhealthy.

There is no safety in numbers with alcohol, just because everyone you know drinks does not make it a safe product, reduce your chances of getting addicted or suffering harm in some way. Whether one person plays Russian roulette or a billion people play the odds remain the same for each person holding the gun. Every pull of the trigger is a separate unique incident and is completely independent of and uninfluenced by all the other triggers being pulled at that time. Just because the people who surround you all appear to be 'in control' of their drinking does not give you licence to assume you will be affected by alcohol in a similar way.

If man is really the most superiorly evolved creature on this planet it does seem strange that we choose to ignore the blatant reality of this drug in favour of a story that holds about as much water as Bill Clinton's insisting that he did not have sex with 'that woman'!

Human beings are motivated by two primary elements. The need to gain pleasure and avoid pain, unfortunately the scales are not evenly balanced and we will do significantly more to achieve the latter than the former. This is why misery, greed and discontentment are rife within most of western society. We will often only go as far as is needed to stop the pain without carrying on in our endeavours to push through to the point of pleasure. Diets fail over and over again for this very reason alone.

Jenny looks in the mirror and grabs hold of the new roll of fat that has slowly developed around her waist. She sighs and looks forlornly at the wardrobe full of clothes that no longer fit. Her weight and body size is making her miserable, but for the moment the pain is not enough to justify giving up the food she loves and associates with a lifestyle she believes herself worthy of. Her current mental assessment is that living without the fine dining, chocolate, cakes and weekend takeaways will be more unpleasant that how she currently feels about her body.

The next day at work something happens that dramatically changes her opinion, as she steps out of the elevator and makes for her cubical she stops short and waits before turning the corner. She hears her name being mentioned in conversation and cocks her head to one side, listening to what is being said. A new intern is asking one of the sales staff who Jenny Taylor is because he has a package to leave on her desk. The salesman, who is rushing out the door on a client call, he is already ten minutes late for shouts over his shoulder 'cubicle 17, big woman, brown hair'!

Jenny's jaw drops open as she gets slapped around the face by the realization that people describe her as 'the big woman' of the office. In my weight loss book Fat Guy Friday this is what I call a threshold moment. This is a point in time when the pleasure/pain balance gets dramatically shifted. Suddenly the pain of being overweight and the associated low self-image becomes massively exaggerated and overtakes the other now insignificant pressure preventing the person from taking action.

Horrified by what she has just overheard, Jenny throws her fried chicken lunch in the garbage and the diet starts immediately. On the way home from work she stops off at the gym and signs up for a yearlong commitment to the dreaded treadmill (despite the fact that she hates the gym, but not quite enough to silence that statement 'big woman, brown hair'). Fitness centres tie you into fixed term deals because they know your current good intentions are going to last six to eight weeks at best. Then you will be banging on their door demanding that they stop debiting your account every month.

Regular gym goers hate January because the treadmills and stationary bikes are clogged up with the New Years Resolution gang; thankfully by March most of them are gone. Although chances are good that they are still paying the club fees because ending a gym membership can sometimes be harder than getting a divorce.

The rabbit food replaces the pizza and Jenny Taylor drags herself to the gym daily for a whole month. That salesman gets at least a dozen evil looks a day as the echo of his description bounces around her wounded mind. Diet cereal for breakfast, salad for lunch and boiled fish for dinner… until one day the jeans that were once too tight slide over her hips. A delightful occasion for any dieter and the next day at work, back in her skinny clothes a few of her colleagues notice the weight loss and make pleasing noises in her direction. The motivational scales take another swing as the pain from the threshold moment dissipates and loses it leverage.

Within a week or so Jenny is allowing herself the 'occasional treat' and skipping the gym on days when she feels a little tired. Within a month she has started to resent the $70 a month the fitness centre takes out of her account, as it feels it is poor value for the odd time she actually makes it past the highway turnoff. It's not long before the pain of depriving herself of life's luxuries far outweighs the trauma of that now distant threshold event. The weight slowly returns until the cycle starts again.

This is what we call the yo-yo diet routine and it's why 95% people who go on a low fat, calorie restrictive diet not only put back on any weight lost, but also adds on average an additional 2-5 lbs.

This universal nature of human behaviour is the reason why highly intelligent and successful people continue to drink a dangerous poison in the name of being social.

All the excuses and reasons they regurgitate to defend their actions are purely a way of balancing the pleasure and pain scales in their head. The fact is while they accept alcohol causes pain in the form of hangovers, depression, driving offences, financial hardship and often irreversible damage to relationships they believe the pain of living without the drug they love will cause significantly more pain. I know this to be true because back when I was a desperately unhappy drinker I could not imagine a life without alcohol. I incorrectly believed that booze was one of the only good things in my life; in reality it was the cause and accelerant to virtually all of the misery. However, if you had tried to take it off me I would have kicked your ass!

Re-experiencing life without a lethal poison constantly sloshing around in your system is like waking up after a terrifying nightmare and realising it was only a dream. During the dark of the night the dream feels real, the scary and unsettling events that played out caused you to physically feel the effects of the nightmare. Inside the dream you cannot see the reality that you are safe under the duvet in your own home.

Only when you wake and look back on the dream from the outside can you see how ridiculous and illogical it was in the first place, you might even wonder how you could believe in the sharp toothed monster that had chased you around your imagination all night long.

When you stop drinking the re-awakening is a slower process than just blinking your eyes open and being back in the safety of your bedroom. Alcohol permeates life on multiple levels and it can take years to realise just how much nonsense you previously subscribed to. In the many years since I last had a drink I have been startled at the behaviour, alcoholic rituals and the very instance of exceptionally intelligent friends and family who still insist the sharp toothed monster is real and I am the imbecile for not believing in it.

One of the most frustrating statements I hear from people I love is 'I only drink to relax'. They will defend this routine with extreme passion and the total confidence that they are in the right. In reality the sense of relaxation comes from the removal of the withdrawal symptoms and nothing else and so if these people didn't drink in the first place there would be no artificial 'relaxation' required at all. However, this is the first illusion of the drug alcohol.

The drinker feels stressed after a hard day at work, takes a drink and suddenly feels better. It is understandable as to why they would connect the two events together and believe that the alcohol fixed their problem – what an amazing liquid! It's harder for the drinker to see that the alcohol used slight of hand to set up the pain they are now feeling a day or so earlier. The kick from the drug alcohol lasts fourteen days and reaches a climax around twenty-four hours after the last consumption. So this means if you drink a glass of wine, for two weeks the drug is going to apply pressure on you to drink again.

The next day you will feel stressed and uncomfortable, most find a reason to explain this such as a hard day at work, unexpected bills waiting for them when they get home or disagreements with friends and family.

Virtually no drinker correctly identifies this sensation as the kick being generated by a drug they consumed the previous day. So the trusty Pinot Grigio is opened and as quick as you can click your fingers the stresses and strain of the day all magically appear to vanish. What the drinker has really done is make a little deal with the devil. They have time shifted the kick forward another twenty-four hours. The devil makes good on his side of the deal and for now they are at peace and feeling grateful to magic liquid that caused the release from the pain.

The first glass leads to another and slowly the anaesthetic nature of the drug takes hold. As I lay on the operating table waiting to be wheeled into theatre the anaesthetist reassured me that I would be asleep during the whole process. Sound quite pleasant doesn't it? Sadly it's not true, general anaesthetic does not induce sleep but rather a reversible coma. Cerebral activity is slowed down to something close to brain stem death, rendering the patient unconscious and completely unaware.

There are no dreams to remember upon waking from a general anaesthetic, as the brain was not capable of creating anything so complicated. Sometimes the doctor will inject the drug and challenge you to count to ten to help them monitor how it is taking hold of your senses. Even the most determined individual rarely gets past a count of five before the lights go out.

We see the same defiance in the face of alcohol. You almost certainly have seen drunk people insisting that they are 'as sober as a judge', offended at the very suggestion that they are smashed out of their minds. Police officers who pull over suspected DUI offenders watch over and over again as intoxicated fools try to fruitlessly demonstrate how in control they are. The moment you drink alcohol you surrender control to the drug, you cannot change the way your body responds to this anymore than you can control gravity.

Alcohol makes the electrical activity in the brain become inconsistent and haphazard as neurons misfire and receptors fail to respond correctly to commands. Simply everyday processes of the human body such as walking and talking become difficult.

The drinker finds their vision is blurred and shifting unnaturally as the brain struggles to correctly process the data coming from the ocular system. As a result walking becomes too challenging. Defeated by something they mastered at the age of ten months they slump into their favourite chair, drink in hand. Speech becomes slurred and inconsistent, the drinker can often be surprised by the noises that are coming from their own mouth in place of the words they were trying to form.

Alcohol regresses the drinker to the capabilities of an infant, without any of the cuteness. They stumble around trying to walk; words are slurred and incomprehensible often reducing the individual to basic grunts and noises. For all intents and purposes you have a brain dead zombie for a companion.

Richards Story:

When Diane walked into his office on her first day as a junior lawyer he knew she was going to be a big distraction. The first time she spoke to him he knew she was the one he would marry. Her striking physical appearance aside this woman was the smartest and most confident person he had ever met in his life.

Richard Baxter, a senior legal partner with a large Cincinnati law firm was responsible for heading up their civil litigation department. As Diane had graduated with honours, specializing in this area she had been assigned to his team. As she was shown into his office on that first morning he wished for two things. Firstly he would have given anything to have gone back in time and picked out a better suit and spent and extra ten minutes in front of the mirror and to have not stumbled over his words when he introduced himself would have been good too.

As he gave his new starter the grand tour he repeatedly caught himself being unusually comedic and looked around to see if there were any raised eyebrows at this strange affable version of Richard Baxter that was on show to the new girl. She smiled politely at his attempts at humour but they both knew you could only be so funny when talking about a photocopier, despite how hard you tried. What floored him completely though was being corrected with a cheeky wink when he reminisced about a famous legal case that had got him interested in litigation in the first place.

"Dawkins versus the Mitel Corporation was 1982, not 1983 Richard", she said with confidence way beyond her position.

He had laughed and disagreed at the time but it didn't stop him Googling the case when he returned to his desk and being exasperated to discover she was right. Beautiful, intelligent and confident, if he could have designed the perfect woman this would be it and here she was just walking into his office out of nowhere.

Diane became Mrs Baxter a few short years later and despite a short career break to have their son, Jack, she climbed the corporate ladder quicker than anyone in the company's long history in Cincinnati. Eventually the only way to progress further was through dead man's shoes or by jumping ship. As the senior partner was her husband the only option was to join a different firm, which she did in the fall of 2010. Diane and Richard occasionally competed against each other in the courtroom and although he would never admit it, Richard prepped his cases just that little bit harder when he knew he was up against his wife. This had nothing to do with one-upmanship; he just knew how good she was.

Richard was down about seven cases to twelve if anyone was keeping count of their courtroom battles.

Of course both of them were keeping count but neither mentioned it. He loved his wife more completely than he ever thought possible and while he still liked to take the occasional victory from her, he loved that she was so consistently kicking his ass. She was his best friend and the first port of call for any advice, not just on legal matters but literally any thing that life threw his way.

Courtroom victories had always been celebrated with Champagne and on the odd occasion when they did fall out he had learnt that from experience that flowers were completely ineffective in pulling him out from the doghouse. An expensive bottle of Bordeaux had proven to do the trick much quicker, especially if served at a Michelin Star restaurant. Without noticing, alcohol had become an intrinsic part of their relationship. It was the automatic default accompaniment to success and failure at work. It was used to celebrate and commiserate in equal measure and more recently for no reason at all.

While Richard's drinking had increased slightly over the years, he had found he simply could not function at work if he crossed the line the night before. Eventually he worked out that a glass he could cope with but beyond that he was going to pay the price the next day. He certainly never drank the night before a big case and this is where the differences with his partner started to show. Diane drank every night without fail, it was the first thing she did when she got home from work and often it came before a hug for Jack and almost always before Richard got a look in. Conversations about their day always took place in the kitchen, Diane with her favourite red in hand as she recounted the twists and turns of her day.

Richard still thought he had the most beautiful wife on planet earth but their sex life had slowly dried up to become a barren desert. It wasn't that Diane didn't want it any more, she had always had an unusually high sex drive and Richard had been more than happy to reciprocate in that regard. The problem these days was the woman that was coming to bed; often hours after he had retired himself was not the woman he had married. Like clockwork, they would both kiss Jack goodnight around eight-o-clock, tucking him into his Spiderman bedcovers usually with a story of superheroes triumphing over evil. Unlike the regular routine they had for their son they had long since stopped hitting the hay at the same time as each other. Richard would read in bed from around ten before switching the light off half an hour later. He would fall asleep on his own but only lightly doze, subconsciously knowing he would be rudely awoken before sleep could begin in earnest.

As Diane would stumble through the bedroom door with the red glow of the LED alarm clock already showing the next day had begun. Richard would blink his eyes open at the commotion and quickly close them again to avoid another pointless incoherent conversation. It was distressing to watch this super intelligent woman struggle to get out of her clothes without it turning into a slapstick routine worthy of Charlie Chaplin. Although this banana skin performance was far from funny, if anything it was a desperately sad tragedy. Sometimes she would make it into her nightdress however other nights the best she could achieve was getting most of her work clothes off. Occasionally even that was too complicated and she would awake fully clothed, Richard would deliberately pretend to be asleep until she got a chance to cover those incidents up.

Eventually she would fall into bed, creating a tsunami of duvet and pillows that even the deepest narcoleptic sufferer couldn't sleep through. Richard still pretended to be unfazed by the disturbance and off in a beautiful land of dreams because he knew exactly what happened next in the nightly pantomime. A heavy arm would land on his chest and clumsy fingers would fumble to undo the buttons on his pyjama top. He didn't need to resist these attempts because she had not once managed to complete the task, it was far beyond her drunken capabilities and she would fall asleep after five or six disastrous attempts, leaving her hand defeated at the scene of its failure. Richard would carefully lift the arm away and turn his back on the sedated zombie – saddened but relieved that finally sleep could begin.

The next morning Diane would awaken and dress for work as though nothing had happened the night before. There was never a trace of a hangover, and the woman he loved was back in the room. She would sit at the breakfast table voicing her social commentary on the news stories flashing by on the television screen. She was funny, articulate and intelligent at this time of the day and how he loved her. So often in the morning as he sat and listened to her he had wanted to just grab her and carry her back to the bedroom so he could make love to the stunning and intelligent woman he met all those years ago. The impending timetable of work always prevented this from happening but he wanted it so much. Come the evening when the opportunity would present itself the women he loved would be gone and the empty, vacant shell that was left behind repulsed him.

In my first book on alcohol addiction 'Alcohol Lied to Me' I make a rather grand claim that unlike supporters of the Alcoholics Anonymous 'Big Book' method to stop drinking I don't have to force myself to stay away from drink. I claimed that I am completely confident in all environments where alcohol is being consumed and I can easily spend time with drinkers without ever wanting to join them. While the latter part of that statement remains true I am afraid the former is now only partly correct. You see lots of my friends and family still drink and I have long since learnt not to preach this stuff – drinkers would rather you urinated on them than dare to challenge their relationship with alcohol.

When I start the evening with bright and intelligent people and end it with bumbling idiots who can barely string a sentence together it actually feels like I am grieving. The person I love has gone; the empty shell that is left behind just reminds me of the beautiful person that once was there. Socially occasions like this are difficult for me because half way though the evening I miss the person that I came in with and all I want to do is leave and go find them.

Drunken people are great company… but only to other drunks! As I have always said 'if you lie down with dogs, you will get up with fleas'. Do you really want to look back on your life and realise you chose to spend years of it under anaesthetic and 'not in the room' while the people who love you grieve for you?

I am sure if you got hit by a drunk driver and spent twenty years of your life in a coma before awakening to realise you are now an old man or woman you would feel cheated by life. And yet here you are consciously choosing this path – why?

If you want to find out just how miserable life can become, try alcohol. I know nothing better to take you right to the bottom of the pit. Because of this, many drinkers like the idea of stopping drinking but at the same time they are terrified of applying permanency to it. The thought of never drinking again is scary, but why?

The problem with the word 'never' is it removes options. It's easy to believe that just because you are living in a democracy that you have freedom. However, I believe true freedom is defined by your ability to make a choice and the more options you have open to you, the more free you are. It's not the walls of the prison that steals your freedom but your lack of option to choose an outcome.

Often when people start my Stop Drinking Course they are a little panicked at the thought of never drinking again. The task ahead seems overwhelming and they pre-decide that they are destined to fail. This is why I tell all my clients that making promises forever are pointless and entirely unnecessary. I don't care if you drink tomorrow, all I care about is that you don't drink right now, and that will always be my stance on things.

The Evil Clown's Disappearing Time Trick

"When everything seems to be going against you, remember that the airplane takes off against the wind, not with it." – Henry Ford

The evil clown certainly has some impressive routines up his sleeve and perhaps one of our favourite is the 'disappearing time trick'. Back when I was a drinker I would frequently beg for this trick to be performed just one more time. Stress was the catalyst for this desire and there was perhaps nothing more likely to send me running to the liquor store than a piece of bad news laying in wait for me at the end of a hard day at work, doom delivered earlier in the day by the mail man. I would use booze to try and cope with these niggles of life and I became so used to being in a semi alcohol induced coma that real life was becoming more and more unbearable, something that I was almost always trying to escape from.

If I came home from work and found the credit card statement lying on the doormat awaiting my attention and then inevitably the attention of my overused check book I would quickly hide the offending envelope under a pile of junk mail and head straight to the liquor store. Whiskey became my favourite weapon with which to slay the dark thoughts in my head and turn off my overactive imagination.

If the credit card banana skin only arrived once a month that would perhaps have been tolerable. Sadly at the peak of my drinking I was spending around $5000 a year on alcohol, which was one of the reasons I had seven credit cards all-creaking at the weight of my growing debt. So the instantly recognisable envelopes of the card companies quite frequently landed on my doormat and made home time an emotional gamble. I argued that I had put in a hard days work and I was entitled to some quality time at home on an evening that wasn't spent worrying about all the bills. Of course my definition of 'quality time' back then meant sitting in a state of near unconsciousness in front of the television until I fell asleep at around 8pm. Yes, my bedtime was earlier than that of most babies and toddlers!

Only now looking back I realise that whether a bill arrived or not was irrelevant I was still going to drink but perhaps just for a different reason. My most convincing argument to myself was the conviction that I wasn't an alcoholic but rather an over-thinker of classic proportions. I simply could not stop my mind from stewing over even the slightest insignificant problem and then proceeding to exaggerate it into a potential disaster.

I used alcohol to pause this action of my mind and time shift the problem forward to the next day. I did this with real issues that actually existed but also with the thousands of imagined problems that I was equally as likely to come up with. Today I tell people that I have been through some horrific things in life but only about 20% of them actually happened.

Of course I should have spotted the first warning sign much earlier, it is fine to talk to yourself but when you start answering back then you know you are in trouble. Us problem drinkers become very good at not seeing the bleeding obvious in favour of a very precariously positioned excuse to ensure we can carry on our love affair with the drug we live for.

When I was a child growing up in the North East of England my granddad Jack would always play the same 'magic coin from the ear' trick every time he saw me. Even as a naive child who adored and looked up to his grandfather it didn't take long for me to notice out of my peripheral vision that the coin was always in his hand from the moment it left his pocket. I occasionally challenged him on the authenticity of the illusion and he would bluster a funny and overacted defence, pretending to be mortally offended at the very suggestion that such a great magician as him would cheat.

All the same, the trick never failed to make me smile and I loved how much joy my granddad got out of performing it for me. I would dearly pay anything for him to be here to day to do it one more time for me. Alcohol delights in a similarly clumsy illusion called the 'The Disappearing Time Trick'. It performs it so frequently because we unfalteringly pretend not to see the very clumsy slight of hand that renders it about as far from magic as you can get.

Drinking to avoid life is perhaps one of the most common reasons I hear to explain an addiction to alcohol. The problem with using alcohol for this reason is rather than it allowing a person to fast forward through time and consciously delete all the troubles and stresses that are currently pressing (as they believe it does). Drinking actually just hits the pause button on the great CD player of life, in the morning when the anaesthetic has worn off the track begins to play from the precise position it was stopped at the night before. Not a single moment of the misery has been skipped; it has simply been frozen and kept fresh for another time. The great 'Disappearing Time Trick' turns out to be complete bunkum, nothing more than smoke and mirrors. Conned by the dark magician, the drinker now has the compound problem of yesterday's problems to deal with on top of the new challenges that will surely present themselves today.

This function of alcohol reminds me of a very funny (and at times painfully sad) movie starring Adam Sandler called 'Click'. In which an ambitious architect called Michael Newman, played by Sandler makes a deal with the Devil, whereby he is given a universal remote control that not only does all the usual things you would expect from such a device such as turning on the television or opening the garage doors but in addition it can also magically control real life too. Michael quickly realises to his delight that with the click of a button he can fast forward through time and even skip events all together.

He stumbles across this apparently miraculous feature of the remote while shivering in sub zero temperatures waiting for his dog to take a leak before bed. The pooch is quite happy sniffing around the yard, oblivious to the encouragement to 'do his business' coming from his frustrated and freezing owner. Curiously Newman points the remote at the dog and hits the fast forward button. In a blur of activity including the rather repugnant cocking of the leg incident he is left gobsmacked by the awesome power of his new device.

As the story unfolds he uses the remote more and more, skipping arguments with his wife, fast forwarding boring visits from the in-laws and eventually incorrectly assuming he was shortly to be promoted at work he asks the remote to jump forward to the day he makes partner at his firm of architects. What he doesn't realise is his promotion was actually a whole decade away and the remote is an intelligent device that learns the behaviour of its owner and then attempts to predict future. The remote assumes that because he has skipped such things as sex with his wife, play time with his kids, Christmas and birthday parties that in the future he will also not want to experience them. It then proceeds to ignore his objections and automatically fast forward him through some of the most sacred and special moments in life.

Towards the end of the movie we see an aged, ill and overweight Michael Newman who is distraught because he has missed his children growing up, lost his wife to another man and has sold his soul to be the most successful partner in the company. He is desperately unhappy and full of regret at throwing away all the moments that makes life really worth living.

I have watched that movie a dozen times, I must have even seen it four or five times with a big glass of whiskey in my hand completely obvious to how the universal remote of that same movie serves the exactly same role as alcohol.

Alcohol makes a deal with people but like a shady insurance salesman it fails to tell them about the small print. It promises to make their problems disappear and while it does make good on that deal what it doesn't mention until it is too late is that the problems will be back the next day but much bigger than ever before. And just like a gambling addict desperately chasing his losses looking for one big payday, now the original problems are exponentially bigger and more painful.

Unable to cope with the avalanche of worry the drinker must now make another significantly larger deal with the devil – the seemingly unbreakable cycle begins in earnest.

Natasha's Story

Natasha Foreman was the life and soul of the office. Not only had she been the senior sales exec for close to a decade, consistently smashing target after target but also she was always the one who pulled the team together. In good times she arranged the celebrations and when they struggled she called for unity and a focus on team spirit. What nobody really noticed, at least initially was that all these seemingly positive attributes to her leadership always created opportunities to drink. If the sales team hit their monthly forecast Natasha would announce that 'On Friday night we are all going out to celebrate'. She introduced something called 'Pink Payday's', this simply meant a crate of pink Champagne would be delivered to the team on the last Friday in the month when they got paid. She sold the idea to the bosses and convinced them to agree to pay for it by suggesting it would create a great atmosphere in building and promote good morale.

If Natasha had only drank on those occasions then all her reasons for arranging such perks for the team would be honorable. In reality Natasha had started building her diary solely around the opportunity to drink. If a big spending client was due to renew a deal it was easy to justify an extravagant liquid lunch on her expenses form. Despite her growing problem she was still as consistent and successful as ever in her career.

She loved the freedom her employees gave her and work was enjoyable but just like most nine to fivers she still wished away the week to get to the weekend. On a Friday night Natasha would say how much she was looking forward to a few days of quality time with her husband and children. In the Monday morning sales meeting she would sit listening to all the stories of great adventures and family outings that her colleagues had had over the proceeding few days and scratch her head in bemusement.

"I don't know how you guys make the time to do all this. We did a supermarket shop and what with one thing and another that was the weekend done. They go far too fast don't you think", she would occasionally say.

The reality is just like medical anesthetic, alcohol steals time. It doesn't matter whether you are going into surgery for a triple heart bypass that takes six hours or the removal of an ingrown toenail that takes six minutes, your perception of the time it takes is the same. From your point of view one moment you are counting to ten and then half a second later a nurse is explaining that you are in the recovery room and the operation went well.

Natasha would start the weekend on a Saturday morning full of good intentions and promises of all the things they were going to do together as a family. Jenny and Brad who were 9 and 7 would bounce off the walls in excitement as they listened to their mom talk about the possibility of visiting the zoo or even travelling up state to the amusement parks. Such fun activities rarely arrived as the weekly supermarket shop had to be done first, where all plans would change in one aisle of the store.

By the end of the liquor aisle Natasha had already decided that tomorrow would be a much better day to make the excursion. She created compelling reasons to defend her procrastination as she wondered from wine to spirits and then onto beer. 'The traffic would be horrendous today', she thought aloud 'and besides it's 11am – half the day is gone already'. To cope with nagging guilt of letting her children down (again) she would gently explain that the trip was postponed and then attempt to repair their tears and disappointment with the sticking plaster of a new toy or a Disney DVD. She would sell them (just as efficiently as she would sell advertising space at work) on the idea of Movie Afternoon… all the family in front of the television with popcorn, chips and dips – now doesn't that sound fun?

The children were easily distracted but still flickers of disappointment remained. Movie afternoon was always a lot less fun that it had sounded in the sales pitch. Sure Buzz and Woody couldn't help but entertain and there was indeed popcorn and chips just as had been promised but mom unconscious on the couch with an empty bottle of wine at her side didn't really feel like she was joining in. The kids would laugh at the slap stick capers on the screen and excited turn to tell their mother about their favorite character, only each time to see that her eyes were closed and she had missed the best bit of the movie.

Natasha would wake alone in the dark, the television now sleeping on 'stand by' and the house in silence. Jenny and Brad had long since been tucked up in bed by their Dad and he had gone to bed alone as usual. A mix of hangover and regret would rush through her awakening mind and as she stumbled up the stairs she would mutter promises to herself, that tomorrow would be a better day. Sunday is all about the family and spending some quality time together. She would lie to herself as she struggled to undress and slump into the bed next to her snoring husband.

Sunday's good intentions would be switched with an activity that allowed for more drinking and before Natasha knew what had happened she found herself sitting in the Monday sales meeting wondering how her colleagues managed to do so much with so little time.

We ask alcohol to perform a magic trick for us. We beg that it makes our problems vanish and sometimes it appears to have done exactly that. In reality David Copperfield never really made the Statue of Liberty disappear and equally alcohol never vanquished our problems, not even for a moment. With breathtaking slight of hand while we watched the magician perform we failed to see the pickpocket at work. Outside our focus a hand dipped into our pocket and rummaged around the contents. There was money, and valuable trinkets in that pocket but the thief took the most precious thing we have... time. It doesn't matter how hard you work, how much you beg or how lucky you get the one thing you can't make more of is time.

"The Evil Clown is always on the other side of the door, waiting. The secret is to never open it", Craig Beck

When you first start to worry about the amount or frequency of your drinking the Evil Clown sits up and takes notice. As most people are aware, getting over the denial of what you are doing is the first and most significant hurdle when dealing with addiction.

For many years, often decades you have used confirmation bias to demonstrate to yourself that you are not doing anything 'wrong' or unusual. You look around at the people you love and trust and they also appear to be using the drug too. You turn on the TV and notice that a lighthearted, family show such as Friends is even sponsored by a brand of wine. Facebook is full of your friends and colleagues all reaching for a cheeky Prosecco. So you embolden yourself with plausible deniability.

For many years you are happy to live inside the lie. The lie is good, the lie makes drinking possible. Of course, despite how it feels, the lie offers you no real protection. Eventually things start to go wrong. Perhaps your finances start to look a bit precarious, your marriage starts to stumble or you pick up a DUI.

There comes a point where you wake up surrounded by the evidence of your misery and finally decide 'enough is enough'. For years you have told yourself that you could stop drinking anytime you wanted to. Well, now here it is. The time you want to!

This is a very dark day for the Evil Clown because you have, for the first time, noticed that his smile is only painted on. You have glimpsed the razor sharp teeth and malevolent grin beneath the greasepaint. The clown always hated you, always wanted you dead but now he is really pissed. Now you are going to make him work harder and he's going to make you pay for that!

No longer will you believe the lie that drinking at your current rate is harmless fun. Those heady days are now in the past, and so the Clown must negotiate a deal with you. His very life depends on it, for a cessation of drinking will lock him in a small, dark prison cell for eternity.

However, the word 'deal' is wrong, because normally when you negotiate a deal with someone, you both hope to get something out of the process. Perhaps neither party in the negotiation will get exactly what they wanted but hopefully they will be able to agree upon a happy compromise.

The Evil Clown has no intention of giving you anything in this deal! He is as smart as you are but with the added advantage of leverage. You see, in an arm wrestle against yourself it would always be a draw. However, because you are now addicted to a drug you are a bit like someone trying to sell their home when everyone in town knows you are broke and are desperate for money.

When you finally decide you want to stop drinking the Clown will offer you a presupposition disguised as a compromise.

A presupposition is a sales persuasion technique that appears to offer the prospect a choice. However, the way the statement is phrased ensures that no matter which option you choose, you get the same result. The statement pre-supposes that you will do as you are told.

For example:

A parent may say to their child on an evening; 'Do you want to go to bed now or in 10 minutes'. The child believes he has a choice and by selecting the later time; he feels he has won a clever victory over his parent. Of course both options lead the child to the same outcome.

So, the Evil Clown will ignore your stated desire to stop drinking and instead ask you if you want to cut down your drinking a lot or just a little bit. It doesn't really matter which option you choose because the Evil Clown is acutely aware that you are incapable of moderating your drinking anyway.

- This is where you start creating silly rules and routines for yourself:
- You tell yourself you will only drink socially and never alone.
- You will only drink wine and never spirits.
- You will only drink at the weekend and not on a week night.
- You will drink a glass of water for every glass of booze.

You should trust me on this; I have been there and done every stupid trick in the book. The Clown sits back and watches this performance with great amusement. This routine is going to keep him entertained for years. Personally I spent at least 5 years of my life in this ridiculous game.

So when people come up to me and say '*do I have to stop drinking, can't I just moderate my drinking*'? I always point out to them that they have been trying to moderate their drinking for years. It's not possible, it never was and it never will be.

How do you know for sure that moderation isn't the answer? Simple, the Evil Clown wants you to moderate your drinking. That's all you need to know! Quitting drinking is easy; reducing your drinking is hell on earth. It's like being on a diet and having a delicious box of chocolates always in your handbag.

When you finally decide it's time to get this attractively packaged poison out of your life. Be aware that the devil is going to offer you a deal. Only a fool does a deal with the devil. There is no possible outcome that can benefit you other than walking away from the negotiation table.

The Evil Clown's Super Self Confidence Spell

"Alcohol is not your friend. The smile is fake, merely painted on. Only the claws and teeth are real", Craig Beck

Back in the nineties I worked on a very successful radio show with a funny guy called Geoff Carter. A larger than life character, who could walk into any crowded room and within minutes have all eyes on him. The king of the jesters, this guy holds court like I have never seen before or since. He oozes confidences and charisma, so much so that when he worked as the road show warm up man for a large radio station in Liverpool, the on-air talent used to complain that he was making them look bad. The audience would scream and cheer for Geoff to come back on stage. This deeply upset the fragile egos of the highly paid presenters who were supposed to be headlining the gigs. Geoff taught me about stage presence and how to work an audience. I don't mind admitting that before I met him I was appallingly average at entertaining and speaking to a live audience.

Spend a day in the same location that Geoff is working and later that day every conversation you overhear will almost certainly be about him. Some of the things I have seen him do in the name of 'entertainment' include running around a five star hotel complex completely naked save for a comedy Halloween mask on, he has more than once or twice managed to get everyone in a bar free drinks by pretending to work for a TV production company and then convincing the owner of the bar that he is scouting for locations for a new show (you really start becoming a hero when you get people free alcohol it appears) and he even won a national UK TV game show dressed as a 10 year old school boy, complete with short trousers and Dennis the menace style sling shot.

Geoff and I never chose to work together; fate just threw us together at the same time. He was already working for a radio station called Magic 999 and I was on the payroll of its larger sister station Rock FM. I had pitched in for promotion to a higher profile shift on my own station and I was excited, if somewhat nervous when one Friday afternoon I was called into the manager's office to be told the news. The Programme Controller of both radio stations was a 6'7" super laid back man called Mark Matthews. I had grown up listening to him on the radio in my hometown of Darlington and I was still slightly star struck at the thought that here I was now working for him. As I sat in front of his office desk he closed the door behind me (always cause for worry I have found, but then if the mail is late I worry).

Skipping the pleasantries and small talk he cut straight to the chase and said he had some good news and bad news. I asked for the bad news first and he told me I had not been given the promotion I wanted. I was devastated as it meant staying on the late evening show, which I was convinced didn't suit me. I felt cheated because I had achieved some impressive listening figures and believed I had served my fair share of time on this anti social shift. Before I got chance to object too strongly he told me that the morning show host on Magic 999 had been fired and I was being moved into that position. I would be working with Geoff Carter and our new double act would start Monday morning at 6am!

Radio is strange like that, quite often two strangers will be picked out and thrown in a studio and told to make it entertaining. Unlike television very little, if any, research or testing is carried out. This makes it quite exciting but similarly it can be quite precarious too. If job security is important to you then I wouldn't recommend a career in broadcasting. If you don't start delivering audience growth within a year then it is you that becomes the guy who is being replaced. This is tough because radio is a very specialist vocation and often in order to get your next line of employment it might mean moving several hundred miles across the country. Not too challenging if you are a single guy but when you are a family man like I was it sucks big time.

It meant selling the home, taking the kids out of a school they loved and telling your wife to say goodbye to her friends (again). In twenty years in commercial radio we moved sixteen times and my children went to five different schools.

The Beck and Carter morning show came together like a perfect storm. My dry and slightly dark observational style humor blended with Geoff's outgoing larger than life personality to create something magical on the air that rarely exists today. Sister station Rock FM was a cash cow and therefore the primary concern of the management which meant Geoff and I had a virtually unrestricted license to do whatever we wanted on the air. Anarchy reigned and as a result this was a dangerous radio show. Dangerous in a good way, you never quite knew what was going to happen next – mainly because neither did we! The audience was huge because many of them simply didn't dare to turn off the show incase they missed something outrageous.

One spring morning on the show, the newsreader, a very studious and serious young man called Stephen Saul was finishing reading the half hourly news bulletin from the third microphone position in the studio. His final article, which is often the more lighthearted story, was about the pending summer solstice. He told us about a group of druids who were going to gather around Stonehenge (a prehistoric monument in Wilshire, England) to re-enact a pagan ritual that would ask the Gods for a plentiful summer. They would dance naked and if successful the country would be blessed with glorious sunshine for the next forty days.

As Stephen finished his bulletin and straightened his tie (he was the only guy in the building to dress this way), Geoff announced to the 70,000 listeners that Stephen would be performing the very same naked sun dance live on the air before 8am. This was a preposterous suggestion because there was nobody more unlikely to agree to such a thing than Stephen Saul. All the listeners could hear as the radio station jingle played and the next song started was Stephen strongly objecting and refusing to have any part of such a demeaning stunt. After much arguing and debating on air he eventually relented and performed the dance but fully clothed. Geoff never forgave him for this and claimed he was solely to blame for the weather being so shockingly bad that summer.

What do you suppose happens to a guy like Geoff when you add alcohol? Let me tell you, carnage happens that's what!

Geoff Carter and I worked in a bubble of unreality. Our lives were completely detached from the normal 9 to 5. We would finish work at 10am each morning, most of our friends had only clocked up the first hour of their shift and ours was already over. We quickly became close friends, partly because the show demanded it and partly because nobody else we knew was available to 'play out' at 10am on a Tuesday morning. Don't let that phrase confuse you; we were not young kids... I was in my late twenties and Geoff a full decade older than me. We were old enough to know better.

Alcohol became the lynch pin of our friendship, it was how we would pass the days together. We were in the pub by 11am most days and we would stay there until at least 6pm. At lunchtime some of the 9 to 5ers from the office would come in and we would welcome them with a raucous cheer. They would stay for their paltry allocated hour and Geoff and I would entertain them. A few of them would return at 5pm after work and find us more drunk but less entertaining, slumped against the bar having been drinking all day. We were generally happy drunks that never caused any trouble and mainly just fell over things and slurred nonsense at people. Unless Garter came out, that was a different story and there was nearly always trouble when Garter arrived!

Garter was the slightly schizophrenic name Geoff had for himself when the drinking went wrong. A character so unlike the real loveable Geoff that it really could be an entirely different person. Garter was an angry guy who was about as unpredictable to hang around with, as it would be to juggle live grenades. Some unknown

115

combinations of drinks caused this alter ego to appear and when it did the day often ended in tears. Garter was irrationally protective of his friends and drinking buddies. Things could turn nasty just because he decided that someone outside our group was looking at us in a 'funny' way. Geoff was an affable but tough guy and I always remember thinking that if anything ever erupted I wouldn't want anyone else by my side in such a situation. However, I would have to counterbalance this admiration with the knowledge that he would most likely be the catalyst to the aggravation in the first place.

Eventually, through exhaustive research and pure dedication to our cause we worked out that two brands of beer had polar opposite effects on him. If he drank Brand A all night long he would end up sitting in the gutter crying his eyes out like a new born baby. However, if he drank Brand B all night he would get aggressive and probably get us into trouble. The trick we worked out was to alternate the brands. It would always have to be Brand A followed strictly by Brand B.

Drinking in this rotation helped us keep an emotional even keel. Of course, at no point did we consider stopping drinking – that would have been unthinkable.

Our relationship will either sound to you like amazing fun or shockingly bad behavior, depending entirely on your personal point of view. I can tell you that it felt fun at the time and I know our nine to five colleagues were envious of our unorthodox lifestyle. Everyday was a different childish adventure that gave us wonderful, colorful and dramatic stories to tell on the air about our escapades the next day. But there is a dark underbelly to this crazy period of my alcoholic life. You see that wacky, zany guy is not who I am, not in the slightest. I am not a reckless idiot who stumbles around getting thrown out of bars. I am not a joke telling comedian who stands on the bar top holding court. This is simply not me and to those who knew the real Craig, this must have been like watching someone descend into mental illness.

Imagine if someone you love suddenly changes all the character traits and personality that you love overnight. They change from being the person you know and feel comfortable with to become an unpredictable stranger. Ask yourself if the guy I have just described to you sounds like the sort of man you would like to have as your husband or the father of your child?

I was supposed to be playing both those roles while I was in this drunken stupor with Geoff. The real Craig is a hardworking, dedicated and creative man who is a solid provider to his family. While the drinkers in the pubs and bars got free entertainment from the banana skin falls of a slapstick, comedy drunk my family lost the man they knew and loved. Alcohol resolutely obeys the laws of the universe and provides a 'yang' to every 'ying'. No matter how stunning the illusion you must always remember that an illusion is all it is! When people say that they drink to feel confident or to help them be more sociable they are falling for just another trick of the drug.

In reality alcohol is just an anesthetic pretending to be something more glamorous. Every aspect of our personality has perfectly evolved to serve a purpose. Interfering with this divine design and changing an element of your character with a chemical can be nothing but a bad idea.

Sure, everyone feels slightly uneasy when they walk into a room full of strangers but understanding that this sensation is not a weakness but rather an automatic response to our evolution from more hazardous times is key to being comfortable with it. Social anxiety and shyness are simply the brain over exaggerating certain risks and creating character traits to protect us that don't serve us in this more modern age. It is only timing that makes this function of the mind feel like a limitation. Back when we were hunter-gatherers and we had to hunt down and kill our food we lived in a much more dangerous and threatening environment. Today we are mollycoddled by our milieu and it is highly unlikely, that as you walk through the mall a savage beast is going to jump out and attack you. And yet the sociophobe constantly experiences the 'flight or fight' sensation in this environment and it feels unwelcome and unhelpful. However, thousands of years ago this very same state of mind would have been a life saving character trait. The person that we today label as being a sufferer of social anxiety would be the most likely to survive an attack.

We all suffer with social awkwardness but on vastly differing levels. In extreme cases it can be a debilitating condition that makes everyday life difficult but even on more normal levels it makes a noticeable impact. Not many people have the confidence to turn up to a party stone cold sober and immediately hit the dance floor. Nightclub dance floors are virtual ghost towns until enough alcohol has been consumed by the customers. It is strange because alcohol really cannot claim to have self-confidence as a side effect of its consumption. What happens when you drink has nothing to do with self-esteem. Alcohol simply interferes with an important part of our brain chemistry that is designed to keep you safe. It reduces your inhibitions and slows down your ability to judge and assess risk. People may say they feel more confident when they drink but in reality they are just more stupid! It feels like confidence because of the environment they are in but if I teleported that person out of the bar and placed them in the central reservation of an eight-lane motorway in rush hour and told them to dodge the speeding cars and cross the road to safety would they still describe what they were feeling as confidence? Probably not, because they would most likely end up confidently squashed under an automobile!

To give you another example of how ridiculous it is to claim alcohol gives people confidence: Imagine for me that you are admitted to hospital for a major operation and the surgeon comes up to the ward to see you before you are taken down to the operating theater. As he talks you though the procedure you notice that his hands are trembling in fear and nervousness. Aware that you have observed his lack of confidence and not wanting you to panic he reassures you by saying 'Oh don't worry I am going to have a good drink before we start'!

Happy to proceed with the operation?

Alcohol creates the illusion of confidence by restricting your field of view. It gives you only a very narrow perception of what is really happening, while hiding the full truth from you. Sometimes racehorses are fitted with blinkers that prevent them from being distracted by events in their peripheral vision. This forces them to focus on what is directly in front of them. Alcohol uses the same principle to block your awareness of the slight of hand going on behind your back. Booze actually creates a form of temporary brain damage that we incorrectly label as confidence. If it were really an increase in self-esteem you would not see the horrific accidents that result from the incorrect assumption of what is happening in the mind. Millions of unwanted pregnancies wouldn't ever have occurred and an equally large number of careers would not have been ruined by some 'confidence' induced faux pas at the office Christmas party.

There is no confidence involved in this trick just the same as the rabbit was never in the hat to begin with. Like a self-help version of Penn and Teller I am here to break the rules and reveal exactly how the alcohol illusion is done.

"Consult not your fears but your hopes and your dreams. Think not about your frustrations, but about your unfulfilled potential. Concern yourself not with what you tried and failed in, but with what it is still possible for you to do", Pope John XXIII (23)

Abraham Maslow is famous for conceptualizing the hierarchy of needs. Postulating that human beings are motivated by the desire to serve common inbuilt prerequisites in a specific order. For example you are unlikely to be concerned with the need for sex if you haven't eaten in a week or have no roof above your head. The needs of self-preservation logically come above the needs for pleasure and comfort

However, the addiction that resides inside you has only one need. That is for you to drink alcohol. It doesn't care how this happens, what emotions you experience as a result of drinking or even if it causes you pleasure or pain. As long as you drink the need is fulfilled.

Additionally the Evil Clown has no memory. You can't appease him by have a good hard drinking session and assuming he will be satisfied sufficiently to give you a break the next day. The clown wants you to drink at every possible opportunity, even if doing so will ultimately kill you. Because the addiction is so focused on this one activity it achieves mastery over it. It knows exactly what buttons to press and how to make the puppet dance perfectly in time with the music. This is how we come up with our belief structures around the drug.

You will have a series of 'go to' phrases to defend your addiction. For example: 'Alcohol helps me cope with life', 'Drinking helps me relax' or 'Alcohol is just one of life's little treats'. On the surface all such statements sound entirely logical and you may feel the urge to challenge my assertion that they are nothing more than lies created by the Clown.

If you are wondering how I know for certain that these statements hold no water, simply replace the drug with another one. We tend to go easy on alcohol because it is legal and sold in convenience stores and supermarkets – hey how dangerous can it be? We assume that cigarette smoking is more addictive and more dangerous to our health and often a drinker will even pat themselves on the back with a cheery 'hey at least I don't smoke or do serious drugs'.

However the reality is, alcohol is significantly more addictive than nicotine and kills someone every 90 seconds. Just because the government endorses it doesn't mean it is safe. This fruit flavored social pleasantry that we believe to be harmless actually kills millions of people every year. Meanwhile the drugs we label as evil, such as heroin, kill a dramatically lower number. Feeling protected because you 'only do alcohol and not the evil drugs' is a bit like being happy you only fell off the 20th floor of the building and not the 30th.

Yesterday I met with an old friend that I hadn't seen for over ten years. Melissa is an estate agent in Yorkshire, England. I have a couple of properties in the UK and she helped me buy and manage them for a long time. She always does a good job for me and a special 'mates rates' price. I decided to sell one of the properties recently and arrange to meet with Melissa on my next visit to the UK. She was supposed to meet me at the property to value it for sale. However, she emailed to say she wasn't well and would send one of her team.

I decided to go visit her at home to catch up and see if she was ok. The woman that answered the door shocked me to my core. A gaunt, ghostly face peered at me. An oxygen tube up her left nostril, attached to a cylinder that she carried under her arm. It was Melissa but not the woman I knew from ten years prior. I couldn't help but take a shocked intake of breath at the sight before me. Before I could stumble around enough to construct a polite question she explained everything I needed to know with one sentence.

"Terminal lung and throat cancer"

I asked her how long she had and she explained that four months ago the doctors had given her three months to live. Melissa was now living on borrowed time.

All her life she had been a heavy smoker and drinker. But do you honestly believe that at her funeral any of her family will take comfort from the knowledge that at least it wasn't one of the 'evil' drugs that killed her?

Stop believing that alcohol can be defended. If you take all those defense statements from above and replace the drug you will quickly and clearly see how devious and dishonest they are:

'Heroin helps me cope with life'
'Taking heroin helps me relax'

'Heroin is just one of life's little treats'.

I advise all my 'Stop Drinking Expert' members to keep a daily journal called 'The Clown Chronicles'. I want them to examine the methods their internal addiction is using to try and get them drinking. When you can step outside the problem and view it from a third person point of view, the insanity becomes more apparent.

To do this, keep a notepad and pen handy. When you get the urge to drink, write down the reason why you want to drink. There will be an explanation and after a while you may even be aware that it appears to be being expressed about you by someone else. For example 'you've had a hard day, you deserve a drink'. This is the voice of the clown disguised as your own internal dialogue.

Next I ask my members to change the drug and play about with the language. Essentially to dissect the command and find the real source of it's existence. Ultimately what you should be able to do is trace every

129

desire to drink back to the primary and solitary need of the Evil Clown... to drink alcohol right now.

For example:

Drinking to cope with life is one of the most common claims of drinkers. However, when you go through the process I just outlined above, you will see that this statement is nonsense.

If you are struggling with the hardship of life and feel sad and depressed about where you are. Why would the logical solution to be to drink a depressant? That would be like going to hospital with a broken leg and being told the cure is to break the other leg too.

It also seems the more depressed you get the more the Clown believes alcohol will help. Take for instance a family bereavement. When you are at the lowest moments of your life, stricken with heartbreaking loss. The clown pops up and suggests what you really need is something that will make you more depressed. The insanity is, we all agree that it's the best thing to do.

Straight after any funeral the dash to the pub begins, where the grieving insists they are just raising a glass to the dearly departed.

I will close this chapter by giving you a challenge. I know that every single defense of alcohol will ultimately lead directly and exclusively back to the need of the clown. If you can come up with any explanation for the beneficial consumption of alcohol that I can't unpick then I will give you a free lifetime membership to my program.

"Everyone has inside of him a piece of good news. The good news is that you don't know how great you can be! How much you can love! What you can accomplish! And what your potential is!" – Anne Frank

I am a chronic worrier, a failing that crosses all boundaries. No aspect of my life is shielded from my tendency to predict doom and gloom. It means if I get a sore throat that doesn't go away within a week I naturally start assuming the worst. My paranoia mixes with my curiosity and Google then helps me confirm that I will be dead within a month.

Hence the saying 'I have been through some horrific things in life but only about 20% of them actually happened'.

It is baffling that for nearly a decade I steadfastly refused to believe that alcohol would or could harm me. I told myself that I was doing exactly the same thing as everyone else, and if I got taken down with something serious then it was down to pure bad luck and nothing else. I only wish I could be as chilled out and at peace with other areas of life as I managed to achieve with this drug. I was aware that alcohol causes horrific illness such as high blood pressure, organ failure and also exponentially increases the risk of getting various types of potentially fatal cancers. Yet despite my propensity to worry I didn't miss a wink of sleep considering this possible outcome of my drinking. This is the power of an addictive drug; it can take the core principles of a person and interfere with them sufficiently to have them do things they wouldn't normally dream of.

Just because I had successfully managed to shove my head in the sand, ostrich style I did not believe alcohol was not doing me any damage. Booze is often called the silent killer because it harms the liver, a vital organ that unfortunately for the drinker contains no nerve endings. This means it can be irreparably damaged with very little symptoms showing. Only when the swelling of the impaired organ begins to press on more sensitive areas of the abdomen does the drinker begin to worry that something may be wrong. By this point the liver could be close to failure and the only way out of the predicament is a transplant. The problem here is one of supply and demand. A new liver means somebody else must die and be registered as a donor. Assuming they can find a liver that matches your blood type in time do you think the drinker is the most worthy recipient? If you had one liver and two patients in need of a transplant who would you give it to if you were told that one of the patients is an alcoholic?

For a decade the 'ostrich syndrome' worked just fine for me until January one year after a particularly heavy festive season. I started to get a dull ache in my right abdomen just under my ribcage. I dismissed it as a hundred different minor, insignificant medical problems from a bit of food poisoning to an intolerance of wheat;

I even considered paying $400 for a food allergy blood test. In summary, I considered everything apart from the obvious, that the 140 units of alcohol a week were destroying my insides the same way alcohol destroys all life at a cellular level.

In February, the dull ache was preventing me getting to sleep and I started searching the Internet for my symptoms. As I scanned the possible reasons for a pain in this region I suddenly became genuinely scared. Website after website suggested liver cancer, liver failure, liver cirrhosis, pancreatic failure, alcohol induced gall bladder disease. The lists went on and on, all horrific illnesses, all caused by alcohol, and many were irreversible. I made an appointment to see my doctor.

In my lifetime I have never had anything seriously wrong with me; I have only ever been to the doctor for a cold or simple chest infection. My past experiences with the medical profession mean I always confidently expect to be told that the condition will clear up on its own, or that a short dose of antibiotics would be all that is needed. This time was different.

I sat in the doctor's waiting room, shaking with fear. I walked in and explained my symptoms. He asked how much I was drinking, I lied and said I used to drink a lot but now I have no more than a glass of wine a night. Can you believe that even at this point I still lied? Of course you can – you still do it all the time! This is the power of this drug we freely hand out to children at celebrations as a 'treat' to make them feel grown up. In honest fear for my life, face to face with a medical professional who was there to help me, I still lied to protect my opportunity to drink. Despite the fact that it was slowly killing me, I couldn't cope with the possibility that it would be taken away from me, so I lied to the doctor.

If you are not from the United Kingdom, let me explain that doctors in England are normally seen at the cost of the state on the National Health Service. Doctor's surgeries are usually over-subscribed and getting an appointment is sometimes difficult. My allocated time with Dr. White was five minutes, behind me there were another seven patents all waiting for their own five minutes. After 35 minutes of examinations and questions, I knew this was going to be a very different experience than I was used to at the doctors.

I still expected, even after all the fuss, for the doctor to nod reassuringly and say "well, I've checked you over and you seem fine, come back in a month if it doesn't improve". Dr White had a concerned but kind face, he looked up from his notes over his small round glasses and said "there is a very real possibility there is something serious behind your pain. I don't have the facilities here to examine you to the level I need to, so I am having you sent to the gastroenterology department at the hospital".

Hospital! Surely not! That is where sick people go; the health service is overstretched as it is, surely they wouldn't waste a valuable bed on someone young and healthy like me? As I walked home, neither cured nor reassured, this was the point when I realized this was not a figment of my imagination. I had possibly seriously damaged my body by selfishly drinking my attractively packaged poison.

I sat at home and watched my children play, and it felt like my heart had been ripped out. Knowing how much I love my family, how could I do that to them? How could I leave my children without a daddy? How could I be so selfish that I would make my children go through the pain of watching their dad's funeral? How could I be so pathetic that I would risk making my wife a single parent, with two devastated children to look after and no income? I am not ashamed to tell you my world was ripped apart that evening, and I cried myself to sleep in a world of self-pity, regret and guilt.

This was my ultimate threshold moment; it altered the balance of all things. For a brief time the pain of continuing to drink was greater than the pain of living without my drug. I stopped drinking for eight weeks and the pain subsided a little. The hospital performed dozens of blood tests and scans, and I was awaiting a liver biopsy because my enzymes were all over the place (a clear indication that my liver was in trauma). The problem with relying on a threshold event to cure your problem is, as soon as the pain generated by the threshold begins to fade, your determination to stick to your goals fades too, and you're back in the hands of good old-fashioned will-power. Let me tell you here and now, will-power is no friend of yours or mine.

At my stop drinking website I explain to members how to break free from the addictive loop of alcohol without having to use will-power. This is the secret to why my method works so well – at no point do you have to force yourself to avoid alcohol. You can comfortably be around other drinkers without feeling like you are being deprived of something.

My propensity to worry probably saved my life because I started to get concerned a lot sooner than most people would of – such is my way. There is a valuable lesson to be learnt by all drinkers of this social pleasantry in a pretty bottle. Just because you feel fine doesn't mean that you are fine. The illusion here is that the playing card is always planted on you long before the trick begins. While the dark magician is busy shuffling the deck and pretending to scan the available cards in search of the one you selected. Alcohol puts on a show for you, keeps you entertained and focused elsewhere until the moment it reveals the card was in your pocket all along.

Sure you could try and outsmart the magician and guess at when he palmed the card into your clothing but the only sure fire way to avoid disaster is not to be the stooge in the first place.

"The more aware of your intentions and your experiences you become, the more you will be able to connect the two, and the more you will be able to create the experiences of your life consciously. This is the development of mastery. It is the creation of authentic power", Gary Zukav

If you want to be a success in life then the advice is to model yourself and your habits on those of others who have achieved success. It is no coincidence that most millionaire entrepreneurs have very similar routines and disciplines in life.

Vladimir Putin is an individual who has been in the media quite a lot of late. Regardless of how the western press portrays him, back home in Russia he is revered and respected. In the UK Theresa May attempted to appear 'strong and stable' by simply repeating the phrase as the answer to any question she was asked. Of course it failed, because the general public are not as stupid as career politicians assume.

Putin owns 'strong and stable' in Russia because he has a set of principles that he won't compromise on. These include a daily two-hour swim, a ban on all technology in his office and a solid commitment to teetotalism.

Part of the reason he doesn't drink is to send a message to the public that alcohol is not necessary or advisable. This is a part of his belief structure and I doubt you will ever catch him with a drink in his hand.

The difference between people who successfully kick alcohol out of their life and those that don't is largely down to mindset and how much passion they have for what they are doing.

In the years of running StopDrinkingExpert.com I have noticed that the people who really manage to escape this drug are the ones who get a little bit obsessed with what they are doing. Living a sober life becomes an essential part of their being. Sobriety becomes woven into the fabric of their outlook; it's as much a part of them as their views on fidelity, friendship and family.

In a way they embrace teetotalism just as passionately as some people take to veganism. It doesn't mean they are never tempted to have the odd bacon sandwich but their beliefs are so firmly embedded that it never gets any further than just that 'the odd temptation'.

The frustration for me as an alcohol therapist is watching people repeatedly trying to use willpower to stop drinking. I see many comments along the lines of 'managed to get through the weekend without a drink' and 'damn, I was doing so well and then I buckled last night and had a beer or two'.

These comments are followed up by well meaning people who say 'don't beat yourself up, you did well to last a week' etc.

Let me be absolutely clear about this 'you did not do well to last a week'. You have failed to understand the way alcohol works. The drug is more than happy for you to go a week without a drink, because it knows you will come back to it even harder every time you do this.

Once you get truly committed to living a sober life then there is no 'getting through the weekend'. There is no battle because you are not forcing yourself to avoid something that you want. Vegan's rarely have to say 'thank God the weekend is over, I made it through without having to eat some lovely meat'. Not eating animals is a part of their personality, it is who they are!

Now, of course I know that meat is not addictive and that is where the comparison falls down. However, what I am trying to tell you is, if you are serious about quitting drinking then you need to make teetotalism a part of who you are.

Decades of drinking alcohol has physically altered your brain. Because of this, you can never go back to moderate drinking, ever! From now on when you drink this attractively packaged poison your brain is going to light up like a Christmas tree.

Despite what some people say, your neural pathways will never return to normal.

With this hard reality you have a choice. You can spend the rest of your life being miserable forcing yourself to avoid the thing you want the most (AA style). Or you can reframe alcohol so it becomes as repugnant to you as a leather jacket is to a committed vegan.

When you are planning your sober recovery from this drug you need to be on your guard for the lies that your addiction will tell you. All these negative beliefs come from f.e.a.r. (False Evidence Appearing Real). For example, many people come to the conclusion that they have an addictive personality and therefore their drinking is not their fault.

They may curse their parents or the medical community, anyone but themselves or their drug. Once you start pointing the finger of blame at an external source you fall into the trap of the drug.

Nobody is to blame for your addiction to alcohol, including yourself. However, you are entirely responsible for dealing with it. Nobody is going to come in and fix this issue for you. Sure, you can get advice and information to make your journey out of the loop easier. But at the end of the day it is only you who can implement and commit to a sober recovery plan.

In reality there is no such thing as an 'addictive personality'. If drinkers all shared such a kink in character then all drinkers would look, act and behave in a similar way. However, attend any rehab clinic and look around at the clients. You will find a completely diverse mix of individuals.

Alcohol hooks all races, genders and social classes. It doesn't care where you live, how many children you have or how powerful you are. Kings and paupers alike are fair game for this drug.

If it really were possible to have an addictive personality then these poor individuals would be addicted to everything. All alcoholics afflicted with this condition would also weigh 400lbs from all the candy they were addicted to. They would be smoking 40 cigarettes a day while sniffing glue constantly.

The moment you come up with a reason to explain your drinking you have a license to fail. Accept no explanation, no reason and no justification. Take responsibility for killing the Evil Clown yourself alone.

"I understood, through rehab, things about creating characters. I understood that creating whole people means knowing where we come from, how we can make a mistake and how we overcome things to make ourselves stronger." – Samuel L. Jackson

Perhaps the least meaningful side effect of alcohol addiction is the financial cost. But please don't misunderstand that statement; this damaging ingredient of the habit still causes immense suffering and misery. I simply believe out of all the chaos created by booze this is the least noteworthy. However, that really is similar to asking which is worse; being stabbed in the heart with a rusty knife or being bitten on the leg by a savage dog? Sure one is obviously worse than the other but neither can be considered a benefit or in anyway a desirable state to be in.

147

Mathematics was always my weakest subject at school and I would avoid doing my algebra homework as diligently as my dog Molly tries to avoid being put in the bath. Drinkers become excellent and dedicated math dodgers; it would only take a few minutes of simple addition to calculate how much they are spending on alcohol. But I will wager most of the heavy drinkers you know have no idea how much they outlay on drink, don't want to know and will very quickly change the subject if you suggest they add it up. Even raising the subject will cause massive pain and as we have already discovered, human beings will always do much more to escape pain than they will to achieve pleasure.

Towards the end of my drinking life I was hit with a disastrous financial problem that threatened to wipe us out. Looking back on that time, it fascinates me how alcohol protected itself from scrutiny and managed to scurry out of the spotlight and into a dark corner out of sight. Hiding away like a dirty rodent while the financial tsunami hit the family. I was working for a large radio station in the North East of England and despite being paid a fairly handsome salary; financially nothing had really changed from when I first started out in the business.

I began in broadcasting as a super eager (read: cheap) 17-year-old boy. I would have done anything to get behind a microphone and that included working for peanuts or less if necessary. Money was not important to me and I suspect my first boss picked up on that rare and most precious of characteristic. I had travelled seven hours for the job interview at Radio Wyvern and I sat nervously in the bosses' office wearing the only suit I owned. He stared at me quizzically from behind his enormous and well-worn oak desk, which was cluttered with every sort of paperwork imaginable. Eventually he spoke and in his distinctive if somewhat comical Geordie accent he told me that I was a terrible broadcaster and he would be taking a huge gamble letting me anywhere near the studio. He suggested that, if anything I should be paying him for the opportunity to gain the experience. I knew at this point if there was an offer of work coming, it was going to be a lowly paid one.

He frowned, paused (as though not entirely sure he was doing the right thing) and told me I would work 7 days a week for $150 per week. I remember wondering how I could be trusted to be on the air seven days a week if I were so terrible at it. I knew I was being taken advantage of but I didn't care, this was what I had dreamed of since the age of twelve. I shook his hand and accepted the job without a second thought. Negotiating the wages on offer didn't even enter my head; I was too worried that if I hesitated and didn't accept immediately the deal would be rescinded.

I started with Radio Wyvern in Worcester a week later. I rented a cheap, damp room in a shared house for $30 a week and drove a battered, ten-year-old car that was tiny but still big enough to hold all my worldly possessions. Despite living like Bob Cratchit, the month was always far too long for the money. A week before payday the cupboards would be bare and I would have to get by on cheap soup and heavily diluted orange cordial.

I cut my radio teeth at this amazing little radio station and despite grumbling about the money and working conditions at the time, in hindsight I realize that the boss of Wyvern really did take a big risk with me. It was a priceless learning experience and if I could go back and do it again, I would, but this time around I would savor every precious moment.

During the year that I worked at Radio Wyvern I presented every show around the clock from the dreaded overnight graveyard shift to taking my place as the youngest morning show host in the country. I learnt my lessons the hard way; I was even suspended three times for making apparently inappropriate comments on air. The yardstick for whether a comment was air worthy or not, was decided by the drinking buddies of the boss, Norman Bilton. If he heard any complaints about any aspect of his radio station in the pub at the end of the day he would come storming into the office in the morning and duly suspend the offending presenter for embarrassing him in front of his friends and neighbors.

I was always a little suspicious about his motives in this regard because I always seemed to get suspended when the receptionist was on vacation. My punishment was conveniently being removed from the air and instead of broadcasting I was forced to work 8 to 6 answering the telephone on the now vacant reception desk. During my rocky time there I also serviced the cars, fixed the vending machine and even cleaned the toilets when my suspension again seemed to match perfectly with the cleaner's sick leave.

As I approached the end of my one-year contract I was being told that there was virtually no chance of it being renewed. To this day I don't know if there was any truth in that threat or if it was designed to manage my expectations of what derisory amount was about to be offered for an extension. Either way it worked, I was scared for my job. I really didn't want to make the long journey home to my parents with my tail between my legs.

With a week to spare I was saved! Another radio station called Mercia FM, fifty miles north of radio Wyvern was looking for a new breakfast host. The managing director, a distinguished looking and well-spoken guy called Stuart Linnell telephoned me and explained that they were considering half a dozen broadcasters but if the opportunity came up, would I be interested? I tried to control my enthusiasm and failed, blurting out that I would love to work for him. He laughed and asked how much I was earning at Wyvern, and then he laughed again.

The next day I sat by the telephone all day, this was before cell phones were anything smaller than a briefcase in size and were exclusively the playthings of the rich and famous. Virtually nobody owned a cell and if they did it was wired into the dash of their Bentley. For Joe Public, when you were expecting a call (normally this activity was the result of giving a girl your number the night before and then waiting patiently for the call that virtually never came) you would literally have to sit in the same room as the telephone and be patient. Occasionally in a panic, you would begin to assume that the lack of a call was down to the phone being broken and you would call someone and ask them to call you back to check it was even capable of ringing. It always lived up to the test and performed its task perfectly, which would make you answer and end the call as quickly as possible.

"It works, thanks mom, gotta go – ring you later'

After a four-hour wait my patience was rewarded, Stuart called to say they saw great potential in me and were prepared to offer me a one-year contract starting immediately. Again I naively forgot to ask about the money and Stuart finished the call by saying 'oh by the way the salary is $15,000'.

Fifteen grand!! Are you serious? Jesus I am rich I thought. I proudly told my fellow sweatshop workers at

Radio Wyvern that I had been poached by another station and they had doubled my money. The fact that doubling my money still meant I earned less than the guys who work on the garbage trucks made no difference to me. I was going to be able to get a new car and actually rent an apartment rather than just a room in a shared house. Wow, this was the big time and I couldn't be more excited.

I enthusiastically turned up at the radio station with my headphones and a box of records. It was much bigger and better resourced than Wyvern and quite daunting for an eighteen year old kid a long way from home. I was the youngest radio presenter at the station, with the least experience and yet I was being put on the highest profile show. Some of the older guys on the station were all set to hate me on sight but I was later told by one of them that when they saw this terrified youngster turn up, looking all timid and in awe of just about everything they simply couldn't bring themselves to hate me.

Nobody really thought I was up to the job and actually they were right. I was massively out of my depth and struggling to get any sort of traction in the audience figures. I later found out that the main reason I had managed to land the job was that I was at least ten thousand dollars cheaper than any of the other options. The boss thought he could take an enthusiastic, young kid and mould him into his perfect morning show host – while saving some cash at the same time. The problem was I had my own ideas about what I wanted to do and sadly most of them were crap. I was adamant that they were genius and would go down a storm – they rarely did. After six months Stuart was losing patience with me and he insisted that I report to his office every morning after my show for a post mortem on my performance that day.

Stuart would pace the room as the recording of that mornings show played out. He would shake his head and tut as he listened to my content and delivery. Occasionally he would pause the tape to tell me how badly I had executed that section of the show. The meeting would end with statements of disappointment and expectations of a better performance tomorrow.

I was beyond depressed, if it had not been my dream for so long I would have quit long ago. Most seasoned morning show professionals will turn up at around 5.30am for a radio programme that starts at 6am. I was getting into the station at no later than 3am in the morning, so desperate to find my feet and impress the boss. Despite how hard I was trying I was getting nowhere and fast. Every day at 10am I got nothing but a frown and lots of sighs from the guy who had employed me.

Down in the dumps, I couldn't cope with another day worrying about work. I stopped at the liquor store on the way home and bought I bottle of whiskey. I sat in my apartment at 11am, the boss's criticism still ringing in my ears as I drank shot after shot until I fell asleep. I awoke, crumpled on my couch to the sound of the alarm in the early hours of the next morning. It wasn't long before this was my preferred way of opting out of life. I would take my daily beating and head home to sleep away the rest of the day. The major problem for a broadcaster who is asleep for eighteen hours a day is you have nothing to talk about on air but your dreams. Some of my dreams were pretty bloody strange thanks to the whiskey, and it might be partly why I was removed from the show a few weeks later.

I was moved to the afternoon air shift, which was a massive relief. There was much less pressure and I didn't have to get up for work in the middle of the night. I stopped the insane drinking and got my life back. I had escaped sliding into alcoholism at this point in my life but I had primed the pump that was going to come back with a vengeance later in my life.

Fast-forward nearly two decades and in the North East I was earning ten times that original amount and yet the end of the month presented the same challenges as I faced at the age of 17. The only difference now was we lived in a big house with a giant high definition television and a serious hi-fi. As far as my drinking was concerned, I was going through my phase of telling myself that I was a wine connoisseur. This was a convenient way of avoiding the truth that I was nothing more than a drunk wrapped up in fancy clothing. I was knocking back the booze every night just like I always had but now I was gulping down $100 bottles of French Bordeaux and even pretentiously recording tasting notes in my journal. I thought I was the king of wine; actually I was just a tosser with a drink problem!

I had got trapped in the illusion that social status and fine wine go hand in hand. If you also believe this let me tell you when the coroner cuts you open on the autopsy slab at no point will he make a note that you were killed by some superb quality alcohol. It makes no difference whether you drink $400 Krug or $5 gut rot – it's the same thing, only one of them is in a very pretty bottle with a whole heap of hype, marketing and social bullshit behind it.

In the United Kingdom we get our self-assessment tax demands in January. I actually think the Inland

Revenue (our version of the IRS) does it on purpose to be spiteful. At some point way back in time, some geeky looking guys at the tax office office had a debate about when would be the absolute worse time to hit people with a massive bill and they unanimously agreed that January would be an awful time to have a tax demand land in the mail box. So without further ado they agreed with a hearty cheer that is exactly when they would mail out the tax demands. With a great sense of achievement and the warm, glowing feeling that they had put a good days work in at the office they all went home to stick needles in the eyes of puppies and kittens.

As the festive season came to an end and the echoes of Auld Lang Syne faded away, I of course made the usual pointless resolutions to cut down on the drinking and actually go to the gym that I had been paying for all year. The Christmas tree was stuffed back into the loft and the 9 to 5 of the New Year began again.

I was ready for the tax bill to land any day, but I was expecting nothing more than a few thousand dollars to be required of me by the taxman and I was quite smug in the knowledge that I had diligently saved roughly that amount away. On the first Thursday of the New Year I came home from work and saw the ominous brown envelope waiting for me on the table. I opened it and unfolded the official looking document, quickly skipping past the boring explanatory text and scanning straight down to the amount due. Surely this was a mistake...

There had to have been a serious computer blip because there were far too many red numbers squeezed into that little box. This was not a couple of thousand dollars this was a couple of tens of thousands of dollars. It was so far off what I was expecting that I was absolutely certain that it was a horrible mistake and I grabbed the phone to lodge an immediate and severe complaint with the tax authority.

Evil Tax Woman: "Inland Revenue, how can I help"
Me: "There has been a mistake with my tax calculation"

ETW: "Ok sir let me look into that for you"

The line went quiet as I was put on hold and I mouthed a short explanation of whom I was ringing and why the veins were popping out of the side of my neck to my wife who had come home at that very moment. As I got half way through a series of expletives about the incompetence of the bloody Inland Revenue the line beeped and the advisor came back on.

ETW: "No mistake Mr. Beck it looks as though there has been a series of errors on your accounts for the last five years and it has just been spotted. So the amount on the demand is back tax for this period on top of what you owe for the past tax year"

Me: "What!"
ETW: "Would you like to make a payment over the phone with a credit card?"
ME: "Jesus, who do you think I am? Only Bill Gates has credit cards with that sort of limit!"

She did not find it funny and neither did I really. My manners went out the window, if the cat had been nearby it would have joined them (cats instinctively know when they are about to be kicked as well as how to always land on their feet). I slammed the phone down on the call center voice and had a mild panic attack, followed quite quickly by a major panic attack. I tried to drink myself to death that night, but sadly it didn't work and I spent the next 12 hours straight in anxiety hell. I paced up and down the house occasionally pausing to shout at the kids or check to see if the cat had come home (it didn't for a 3 weeks). This paralysis lasted for three days until my mood lightened and I eventually decided we could fight our way out of this mess, but it wasn't going to be easy.

We had one of those awkward middle class house meetings where I explained to the children that serious cutbacks were being made. These days when politicians want to take your house they call it an austerity measure, doesn't that sound pleasant? I didn't bother coming up with any softening techniques;

I went for the harsh reality approach… games consoles, satellite television, vacations and all other non-essentials were either being turned off or put on eBay. As the children howled and screamed I also landed the bombshell that we needed to move out of our lovely home and find somewhere much, much cheaper to live.

Our gorgeous, 'brand new' three-story town house was traded in for a tatty, badly decorated semi detached shed that smelt of what I can only describe as 'old people', that unsettling and slightly nauseous odor of pickled cabbage and death that hits you as you walk into any retirement home. It was quite frankly disgusting but it was less than a third of the monthly price of the town house and sacrifices had to be made.

Our first night in the new (but old) house was uncomfortable. The big plasma screen television had gone in what will forever be known as the 'Great Tax Bill Massacre' and we huddled around a battered old-fashioned TV that my mom had leant us. It was only a tiny screen but the set weighed the same as a baby elephant. As the screen flickered to life and demonstrated the true glory of low definition technology, the room filled with the noise of family members sighing in abject disappointment. I sighed too in agreement and poured myself a large glass of red wine from the bottle that was always in reach of my new, horrible old man's arm chair.

Right there in that sentence is the reality of what a drinker will do to the people he loves before he will give up his drug. The kids lost toys and games that they loved, my wife moved from a home she adored and for the next eighteen months we lived like paupers. Hell I even gave up my television – I loved that TV! At no point did my alcohol consumption even make it onto the negotiating table. Sure I opted for the cheaper booze and fine dining with accompanying wine was long gone but I was still downing hundreds of dollars a month in alcohol... thousands of dollars a year on a drug! Today I wonder just how much more misery and debt would have had to be piled on us for alcohol to come under the spotlight.

The honest answer is I don't think there would have been enough pain to stop my love affair with alcohol. When you are inside the loop you believe all sorts of nonsense. People struggling with financial trouble all over the world will claim of alcohol:

- It is my only pleasure in life, if I have to give this up then I might as well be dead.
- I need it to get through the challenges I am going through.
- I wouldn't sleep at night without a drink at the moment.

When you manage to escape the cycle and can observe the addiction from the outside, it is so clear to see that alcohol not only makes every problem ten times worse but in the case of financial hardship it has a compound effect on the original problem and then adds a heap of misery on top for good measure.

The average drinker who joins my online stop drinking club is spending around $3000 a year on alcohol! That might sounds a lot, and the tendency of any drinker is to assume they are no where near that amount but $3000 is less than ten bucks a day and so if you are one of those people who drink a bottle of wine a day plus a bit more at the weekend then you are way over that figure. Let's keep the glass half full (excuse the pun) and we will stick with the average. Every person I have ever spoken to has agreed that they could find something important to do with $3000 dollars.

If I gave you that money today and told you to go blow it, what would you do with it?

- Maybe take the kids to Disneyland?
- Put it towards a new car?
- A romantic vacation?
- Put it towards the college fund?
- A medical bill or procedure?
- Pay off a credit card?

Whether you would use it to make life bearable or to simply add pleasure for you and those you love. That money is there and waiting for you to do any one of those things. You don't have to ask your boss for a raise, work overtime or change job – it is already yours! To get it, all you have to do is step outside your current situation and see that alcohol is not your friend, helping you deal with a difficult life but rather your enemy, deliberately stealing all those wonderful things from you and your family.

My challenge to you is to put this book down and do the exercise that 95% of drinkers refuse to even consider. Sit down and honestly work out how much you spend on alcohol in a year. Make sure you include those lunchtime drinks with clients, weekend binges and the special occasions such as Christmas and birthdays. Those times when you treat yourself to much more expensive poison than usual. Come up with you golden number and then think about what you would do with that money if somebody gave it to you in a lump sum today.

Next take that image, whether it is the trip to Florida you have always wanted to take or clearing the debt that just won't leave you alone. Get on the Internet and find an image that represents that aspirational item. Print it out and stick it on the refrigerator or bathroom mirror. Somewhere where you will see it everyday. If you ever take that image down without having completed the goal you will know that alcohol still has a hold over you.

The Addictive Personality Illusion

"Life is a series of addictions and without them we die",
Isaac Marks

You would not believe how many times I have heard someone tell me with unbreakable certainty that they have an 'addictive personality'. This they go on to explain is why they are so hopelessly hooked on booze.

Addictive Personality? There is no such thing, let me explain why!

These days we get obsessed with giving labels to things. You can no longer find a naughty child anymore; they are all suffering with this disorder or that disorder. The word addictive has become so over used that it no longer has any real meaning. We talk about a new TV series being addictive; apparently we are surrounded by sex addicts and serial pornography users.

The fact is we like doing certain things! We enjoy being entertained by a well-written TV series and there is nothing wrong with that. It doesn't mean we are hopelessly out of control because we watch an entire box set in a weekend.

The phrase 'an addictive personality' doesn't make any sense. It implies that something impossible is being achieved. That the addictive nature of a substance is being generated by the user and not the substance itself.

If some people were really said to have an addictive personality they would, therefore be addicted to everything. It wouldn't matter whether the substance in question was addictive or not, because the affliction would be being generated internally within the user. People suffering with an addictive personality would be hooked on potatoes and mayonnaise. They would all be 400lbs from their addiction to food and most of them would be dead by the time they are 20 from all the cigarettes they smoked and all the glue they sniffed constantly throughout the day.

Drinkers use the phrase 'addictive personality' because the Evil Clown gives it to them as a justification to carry on drinking the poison. We tend to become the label we apply to ourselves. But we can also manifest our beliefs into the lives of other people through our belief system and corresponding actions.

The first psychologist to systematically study this was a Harvard professor named Robert Rosenthal, who in 1964 did a wonderful experiment at an elementary school south of San Francisco.

The idea was to figure out what would happen if teachers were told that certain kids in their class were destined to succeed, so Rosenthal took a normal IQ test and dressed it up as a different test.

"It was a standardized IQ test, Flanagan's Test of General Ability," he says. "But the cover we put on it, we had printed on every test booklet, said 'Harvard Test of Inflected Acquisition.' "

Rosenthal told the teachers that this very special test from Harvard had the very special ability to predict which kids were about to be very special — that is, which kids were about to experience a dramatic growth in their IQ.

After the kids took the test, he then chose from every class several children totally at random. There was nothing at all to distinguish these kids from the other kids, but he told their teachers that the test predicted the kids were on the verge of an intense intellectual bloom.

As he followed the children over the next two years, Rosenthal discovered that the teachers' expectations of these kids really did affect the students. "If teachers had been led to expect greater gains in IQ, then increasingly, those kids gained more IQ," he says.

You get what you think about, most of the time. Thoughts really do become things. I once coached a millionaire entrepreneur who believed he was ugly and would never find a beautiful woman to be his wife. We sat talking for half and hour and he explained how he had started with nothing, coming for a broken home with absolutely no opportunities around.

He explained he had fought hard and invested in himself. He had taken a lot of risks along the way but through sheer passion, determination and commitment he had built a business empire that now employs thousands of people. He finished his story and said 'so as you can see I need no help with money. I have all the money I will ever need. My problem is I am just so unattractive to women, I always end up with people who are no good for me or who treat me badly'.

It took me a whole weekend working with this guy to demonstrate to him just how valuable a man he was. He had personality traits and strength of character that most women would find totally irresistible. He had integrity and moral fiber that women can spend a lifetime looking for in a man.

On our final night together he saw a woman he was attracted to. He looked me in the eye and said 'I just want to try something', and then he got up from our table and walked over to her. After a few seconds he had her smiling and laughing. In total he chatted with her for no more than ten minutes before he came back to me with a scrap of paper in his hand. Written on the paper were the name Zoe and a cell phone number. He couldn't believe what had just happened to him, but I could – I had seen it happen many times before.

So what happened to this guy, did he become attractive to women during our time together or had he always been attractive but deliberately sabotaging himself to ensure reality fit the belief structure?

The Evil Clown knows you can stop drinking any time you want to. So he must convince you that you are not to blame and cannot accept responsibility. It's not the blind man's fault that he is blind and there is nothing he can do about it. Equally the clown suggests; it's not your fault that you have an addictive personality and there is nothing you can do about it. So you might as well drink and accept it.

There is no such thing as an addictive personality, it's just another excuse, and another license to fail printed by the Evil Clown living inside your head.

Does life without alcohol suck?

"Today I choose life. Every morning when I wake up I can choose joy, happiness, negativity, pain... To feel the freedom that comes from being able to continue to make mistakes and choices - today I choose to feel life, not to deny my humanity but embrace it", Kevyn Aucoin

This question came from a couple of my Stop Drinking program members who were chatting on Facebook. They were agreeing with each other that a life without alcohol appears to be dull.

I can completely understand this thinking. I probably spent five years of my drinking life avoiding dealing with my addiction due the same sort of thinking.

Alcohol was so deeply ingrained into my life that I simply couldn't see how I could function without it. I worried that I would have no way to relax, no way to socialize and even no way to get to sleep of a night.

The only thing I can tell you, having been on both sides of the coin is this. The worry that life is less without alcohol is just another illusion of the drug.

You have to marvel at the power of this poison. It has the power to make you look at black and call it white. Alcohol brings nothing but misery and suffering and yet somehow it manages to persuade you that you can't live without it.

I wish I had the words to describe the difference between my happy sober life now and the fat, zombified existence that I insisted I 'enjoyed' as a drunk.

It's a frustrating problem for me personally, because I speak for a living. I spent over twenty years as a professional broadcaster and yet I can't describe just how much better my life is without alcohol. Perhaps the words don't exist!

I have mentioned repeatedly about the obvious downsides of alcohol addiction. The fact that it steals your money, time, health and relationships.

What I have never talked about before is the damage alcohol does to your spiritual health.

Wait… before you run away because I have gone all-spiritual on you. What I mean by spiritual is a inner state of peace and happiness. We as a species get a little confused between happiness and fun. I believe happiness comes from within and fun is just an external input.

Whether you are religious, spiritual or just open to meditation the fundamental goal remains the same: To reduce the ego and spend more time in grateful appreciation of the present moment. True peace and happiness only exists in the 'now', never in the future or past.

Alcohol prevents you achieving this aim. The alcohol addict is rarely in the moment. While they are consuming alcohol they are sedated and prevented from being fully aware by the drug. When they are not drinking they are plotting and planning when they will next be able to do so.

I recorded a video to go along with this chapter. I went to the beach where I got married fifteen years ago. The stunningly beautiful location I have been with my children and family many times in the past.

Until I went back to make the video I can honestly say I have never really been there before. Let me explain that statement, sure I have been there physically, many times before. However, I was never really present mentally to appreciate the beauty around me.

All I was thinking was 'yes very good, when can we go back to the hotel'. It's not that the hotel was so amazing that I couldn't bare to be parted from it. I think you know why I was so desperate to get back to the hotel.

Finally when I stood on that beach sober and allowed myself to really experience the beauty of the place, a wave of peace washed over me. It almost brought a tear to my eye – a powerful moment I allowed alcohol to steal from me a million times over.

If you want to be sad live in the past, if you want to be worried live in the future. Happiness and true peace exists only in the present moment.

Alcohol will do everything it can to prevent you staying here.

What you will find is that after six months of sober living, you will look back on the question of whether 'life without alcohol sucks' and laugh until you are sick.

There is nothing I can say to really persuade a drinker of this, all I can do is challenge you to experience it. I know you will come back to me full of shock, excitement and pure joy having experienced first hand what a sober life feels like.

The Ugly Tree

"In the midst of winter, I found there was, within me, an invincible summer. And that makes me happy. For it says that no matter how hard the world pushes against me, within me, there's something stronger — something better, pushing right back." – Albert Camus

I am a passionate follower of the sport of Rugby League, which is played predominately along the M62 corridor in England, a little in France and also heavily across Australia, where it is known as the NRL. A few years ago I became a match commentator for a radio station based in the North West of the United Kingdom. I didn't get paid anything beyond expenses but I got to watch the matches for free and from the infinitely more comfortable press box rather than shivering in the stands with the rest of the fans.

Despite twenty years in broadcasting I was still very much a beginner at the extremely difficult job of live sports commentary. The professionals make it sound easy but continuing to talk and paint mental pictures for your audience, who do not have the benefit of being able to see what is happening for the full eighty minutes is a tough challenge. As a newbie for the first half of the season I was only allowed to be the match summarizer. Effectively this means the secondary voice that the main commentator will cross to when he needs another opinion or simply wants to take a break.

One freezing cold Friday night in Leeds, Yorkshire I was in the press position alongside a very experienced rugby commentator called Mark Wilson. We had our headphones on and lip microphones in place ready to describe the action about to begin on the field of play. Leeds Rhinos were playing host to the away team the Wigan Warriors. The hooter screamed out the start of the match and Mark was off, waxing lyrical about the awesome beauty of the slide tackle technique being incorporated into the game by the Warriors. It was at this moment that I felt hopelessly out of my depth again and totally in awe of Mark and his ability to perfectly summarize what was happening on the field.

Sitting on my couch at home, I considered myself to be the worlds best rugby commentator. Now here in the spotlight of live radio I realized I had only been no better than any other sports fan, shouting abuse at the referee from the comfort and safety of his own lounge. With a microphone in front of me I suddenly realized I would have to keep virtually all of my ill-advised opinions to myself for risk of being sued for slander or defamation. I certainly couldn't suggest that the referee had the mental capacity of a chimpanzee and the eyesight of a particularly shortsighted fruit bat. A mild panic came over me as I wondered what, if anything I could say. I got my opportunity to find out a few seconds later!

Jamie Jones had completed the tackle for the Rhinos and had left a Warriors player nursing a busted nose. As the injured played received treatment from the on field medic, Mark took the opportunity of a break in play to pass the commentary over to me while he took a slurp of coffee.

Mark: "So Craig what do you make of that from Jamie Jones"
Me: ... (silence)
Mark: "Jamie Jones with a bone crunching tackle there, what do you think?"

Mark raised an eyebrow to me that simply said 'talk you donkey'. He held his coffee cup suspended in mid air, desperate for me to start talking so he could take a well-deserved sip of the warming liquid. As a Wigan Warriors fan I couldn't think of anything broadcast worthy to say about the tackle. I didn't know what I thought about the technique on display because I was so pissed that Jones had taken out our best player.

Me: "Well Mark I think Jamie Jones must have fallen out of the ugly tree when he was a kid"
Mark: (Spurts coffee onto the control panel)

Me: "And by the looks of his face I would say he hit every branch on the way down"
Mark: "Erm… the comments of Craig Beck there everyone. Certainly nothing to do with me."

He returned to commentating on the game and he didn't seek my opinion again until later in the second half. What I didn't appreciate is that after the game we would have to go interview the players face to face. If you want to know the meaning of fear, try interviewing a 6'7", 300 lb rugby player who has just lost the match and has now heard that you have described him on live radio as being the ugliest man on planet earth. It is nothing short of a miracle that I am here to write this book.

The fact is if you play a contact sport like Rugby you are going to get hit with the ugly stick a few times. I once interviewed a full back called Shaun Briscoe about the state of his nose (it really is a wonder that I can still walk). Shaun is a good sport and explained that he has had his nose broken seven times in his career. This unfortunately has left him with something that doesn't really look like a nose at all; it's a strange zigzag that crumples to a stub at the end. It looks more like a squashed tomato than a nose if you ask me (and he didn't). I asked if he would consider cosmetic surgery to repair the damage he replied that there was no point while he was still playing professional rugby. His plan was to live with it until his career was over and then get it fixed.

Another illusion of the dark magician is the transference of beauty. How many people wake up on a Sunday morning lying next to a dog ugly stranger, wondering where the stunning goddess or Greek Adonis they met the night before went to? I am sure nothing so unsavory has ever happened to you but rest assured, beer has been helping ugly people to have sex for hundreds of years – God bless it!

By now I hope you can see why I compare alcohol to some twisted magician. This substance, that we adamantly insist is nothing more than a social pleasantry can make us believe things have vanished before our eyes, it can steal our money without detection, make us see things that are not there at all and even makes us believe someone who looks like Kathy Bates is a gorgeous cat walk model who must be seduced!

Alcohol may make people appear to be significantly more attractive than they really are but while it is busy making silk purses out of sows' ears, the drug is actually taking payment for this trick directly from you. Drink alcohol heavily and you might as well play rugby because the ugly stick is coming to give you a good whacking either way!

Alcohol's effect on your skin is similar to its effect on the rest of your body: it steals the good hydration and leaves the bad (dryness, bloating and redness). When you drink alcohol, it hinders the production of vasopressin, an anti-diuretic hormone. This causes your kidneys to work extra hard to remove excess water from your system, sending water to your bladder (and you to the restroom!) instead of your organs. Don't forget that your skin is the largest organ in the body, and drinking a lot of alcohol leaves it dehydrated.

When skin is dry, it is much more likely to wrinkle and make you look older than you are. Alcohol also robs your body of Vitamin A, which is essential for cell renewal and turnover, so your skin could take on a dull gray appearance. Staying hydrated will obviously have opposing effects: smoothing out wrinkles, leaving your skin looking bright, young and fresh. Drinking water is the only way to combat the drying effects of alcohol, hydrating from within.

Being so depleted of vital nutrients, electrolytes and fluids, your skin often shows signs of bloating and swelling. When you're lacking what you need, your body will store whatever it can get, wherever it can, and any water you take in will cause your tissues to swell.

Alcohol can also affect pre-existing conditions like rosacea, causing it to worsen or flare up more often.

189

Alcohol increases your blood flow, often causing blood vessels in your face to dilate (sometimes permanently) and often burst, leaving behind broken capillaries and red spots that are difficult to get rid of.

When you drink alcohol, it's broken down into acetate (basically vinegar), which the body will burn before any other calorie you've consumed or stored, including fat or even sugar. So if you drink and consume more calories than you need, you're more likely to store the fat from the Twinkie ™ you ate and the sugar from the Coke ™ you drank because your body is getting all its energy from the acetate in the beer you sucked down. Further, studies show that alcohol temporarily inhibits "lipid oxidation" in other words, when alcohol is in your system, it's harder for your body to burn fat that's already there.

Your body has a set number of calories needed to maintain your weight. This need is based on your height, weight, age, gender, and activity level. When you consume more calories than your body needs, you will gain weight. Alcohol can lead to weight gain from the calories it provides and by causing you to eat more calories after consuming the alcohol.

It's easy to forget that you can drink as many calories as you eat. In fact, some drinks can have as many calories as a meal! Check out how many calories you can get from your favorite cocktail below. Remember to check the serving size and to add the calories from any juice or soda that is combined with the liquor:

Alcoholic drink	Calories
Beer, lite, 12 oz.	100
Beer, regular, 12 oz.	150
Frozen daiquiri, 4 oz.	216
Gin, 1.5 oz.	110
Mai tai, 4 oz.	310
Margarita, 4 oz.	270
Rum, 1.5 oz.	96
Vodka, 1.5 oz.	96
Whiskey, 1.5 oz.	105

Wine spritzer, 4 oz.	49
Wine, dessert, sweet, 4 oz.	180

The next time you reach for a cocktail before your meal consider if it's worth the weight that you could be gaining from it. Research has shown a 20% increase in calories consumed at a meal when alcohol was consumed before the meal. There was a total caloric increase of 33% when the calories from the alcohol were added. Along with the increase in weight you can have an increased risk to your health because of where you gain the weight. A study of over 3,000 people showed that consuming elevated amounts of alcohol is associated with abdominal obesity in men.

Many people joke about this being a "beer belly." Unfortunately, a "beer belly" puts you at an increased risk for type 2 diabetes, elevated blood lipids, hypertension, and cardiovascular disease.

The late-night munchies are often associated with a night of drinking. Have you ever realized that anytime you drink alcohol you are hungrier or you end up eating more than usual?

Studies have shown that in the short term, alcohol stimulates food intake and can also increase feelings of hunger. Having your judgment impaired and stimulating your appetite is a recipe for failure if you are trying to follow a weight-loss plan.

Greg's Story:

There is probably nowhere else on planet earth other than Beverley Hills where being crowned, as the end of year prom king or queen is a more significant an honor. Twenty-five years on Greg Campbell stared at the high school reunion invite in his hand and was teleported back to that amazing night. Beverley Milner was his queen and she looked every bit the part. Long flowing blonde hair, a tiny waist, perfect smile and the knowledge that just about every guy in the year would have given his left arm for a date with her. Naturally she was the head cheerleader for the mighty black and orange and spent match days cheering on Greg and the team. At the time Greg thought nothing of the six-pack that came as natural by product of being quarter back for the Normans. He had heard his name shouted and screamed more times that football season than any he could remember. The adoration had peaked when they had steamrollered Culver City against all odds and expectations. The Centaurs should have nailed them that day but something just clicked, the team flowed perfectly and they left the field as local heroes.

Had it really been twenty-five years since he walked down that garishly decorated staircase with his queen on his arm, as the rest of his classmates cheered and applauded? The years had flown by and exactly as predicted Greg had gone on to achieve astounding things.

He had tucked the invitation into his sports coat before jumping into the car for his usual 7am commute into the office. He worked hard but the fruit of his labor was easy for all to see. He would deliberately start early in the morning so he could beat the rush hour traffic and spend an hour at the desk of his business before the team got in at nine.

He had set up a small tech business while he was at SFSU and while it was initially just a crazy idea that turned into a hobby and was a very slow build, it eventually went on to employ fifteen designers and developers before he sold to Microsoft in late 2008. The deal had taken his baby away from him and for a while he didn't know what to do with himself. The flipside of that had turned him into one of those web millionaires overnight. He really didn't need to work again for as long as he lived but Greg rarely worked because he had to. He had never had a proper 9 to 5 job his whole life. He did what he was passionate about and money just seemed to be a derivative of that.

The other benefit of missing the morning rush and being his own boss meant he was always home in plenty of time to pick his kids up from school. Jacqui and Brett, 7 and 9 were the apples of his eye and he loved seeing their excited faces as the school bell rang and released them into his open arms. He was acutely aware that mom's outnumbered the dad's on the school run by more than ten to one. Many would say he was a lucky guy but Greg didn't believe it for a moment. It was hard work and dedication that had got him into this position and while he was grateful for his lot in life, he put very little of it down to luck.

Gregory Campbell was proud to be a self-made success story; he had most everything that every other guy dreamed of and the self-confidence to go with it too. Certainly not a reckless risk taker, but he would certainly try anything once, anything apart from that reunion it would seem. The invitation remained tucked into his coat pocket but now it was a little dog-eared and crumpled from over inspection. He had repeatedly grabbed it from its dark hiding place with the intention to make a decision once and for all. For nearly a week he had dodged the dilemma and the still the thought of confirming his attendance sent a shiver down his spine. He desperately wanted to go, he wanted to see Beverley again. Of course he knew what she looked like these days, everyone did. Beverley Thornton as she had become was the news anchor on the local TV channel. She still looked stunning, although how much of it was cosmetic surgery, TV make up and clever lighting he didn't know. He wanted to walk down that balloon tied staircase again with her on his arm and just for an evening pretend he was still Greg the hero of the school, Greg the record-breaking quarterback, the guy all the other guys looked up to.

Back then he weighed 196lbs of pure muscle, his abs looked like a washboard. The girls would run their hands up his arms just to feel his rock hard biceps and perfectly chiseled shoulders. As he walked back to his automobile, the kids enthusiastically leading the way, he glanced down at his shoes. They may well have been made from the finest Italian leather but he couldn't even see them. He only had his continued forward momentum to confirm he even had legs. There was nothing visible from his point of view these days, save his painfully swollen gut hanging unattractively over his belt. He hadn't dared jump on the weighing scales in an awfully long time but he was guessing his weight was more like 260lbs now, and without a single muscle in sight.

Along with the cars, houses and vacations all over the world came a wine collector's paradise. Submerged in the basement of his Beverly Hills mansion was a custom built, atmospherically controlled wine cellar that Greg would show off to anyone with even a passing interest in the 'good stuff'. The pomp and ceremony of selecting a fine bottle of wine (or two) to accompany dinner wasn't just reserved for guests. Greg loved to walk the rows of outlandishly expensive French reds before choosing a dust-covered bottle that had probably remained untouched for decades. He had long since stopped counting how much he was spending on the vino. He told himself it was an investment, although somewhere deep down inside a small voice shouted 'bullshit' repeatedly.

Greg told himself that he worked hard and he deserved to relax in style. The problem is over the last decade or so this self-adulation had become a nightly occurrence. He had long since given up finding a social excuse to break out a bank busting Bordeaux or a bottle of aged Rioja that cost more than most people's mortgage payment. Once the kids were in bed Greg would drink, there was some TV involved too but the primary activity was sitting on his ass and drinking until he collapsed.

He had put on a couple of pounds a year until five years ago; he hated being the big fat guy in the expensive gym. Those places in Beverley Hills are strictly reserved for the pretty people and despite his financial success he was starting to feel like the proverbial bad penny every time he returned to the treadmill. Since giving up on exercise his weight gain had accelerated and these days when the kids drew a picture of daddy it always started with a massive circle. As his weight had gone up, his health had gone downhill with equal momentum. The evidence of his drinking was visible for all to see. His nose, once in perfect proportion to his other handsome features was now bulbous and covered in a patchwork of thread line veins all threatening to rupture at the same time. His eyes had lost their sparkle and dark circles under them gave him a hangdog expression that wouldn't go away no matter how hard he smiled.

The colossal weight crushing his joints was only half the reason he struggled with stairs and had never played ball with his boy. Earlier in the year his very expensive doctor had diagnosed pancreatitis and advised an immediate cessation to all alcohol and rich foods. Greg had compromised by donating his Port and Sherry collection to grateful friends and cut out the fatty cheese. He would make great show of turning down the cheese board for health reasons at evening functions but that was as far as he was prepared to go.

He avoided further rebukes by avoiding the doctor at all costs.

At work, he had managed to surround himself with yes men and staff too smart to say anything but what he wanted to hear. When Nicola on reception commented on how well he was looking he would nod and agree. Rachael his secretary knew her boss didn't want to be bothered with something as inconvenient as the truth when it came to his appearance and so she obliged with the faux pleasantries and he reciprocated in turn. Despite it all, that annoying and persistent voice from deep within was still there reminding him of reality. He knew what the reunion would be like; he had experienced something similar recently.

The year prior he had been attending a conference in Texas and a knock on his hotel door as good as ruined the whole trip for him. An old friend from high school, a guy called Brian Taylor had recognized his name and company on the seating plan for dinner and had gone on a mission to track him down. Expecting the cheery ratatat tat on his suite door to be room service, Greg had flung the door open with nothing but a bath towel struggling to wrap itself around his beer keg of a waist. No smartly dressed yet expressionless bellboy stood waiting with his whiskey. Instead there was Brian Taylor in his tux; Greg watched his face drop from a cheerful 'look who it is' expression. In what felt like slow motion it went from shock through horror and disgust back to a fake 'happy to see you' smile... but try as he might he couldn't sustain it.

"Jesus Greg are you ok?", Brian had asked, completely forgetting to even say hello first.

With that thought sticking knives into his very soul he grabbed at the invite in his pocket and ripped it in half.

Fake Friends & Misguided Fish

The two most misused words in the entire English vocabulary are love and friendship. A true friend would die for you, so when you start trying to count them on one hand, you don't need any fingers. Larry Flynt

When people visit my website and sign up for the free downloads, I ask them what they are most worried about, when it comes to quitting drinking. The single most common reply is "I am worried about losing my friends".

I would love to tell you that all your fears are misplaced and nothing is going to change when you stop drinking poison for fun. However, the reality is the way you look at your life is going to take a dramatic shift. What seemed important before will be revealed to be mere triviality. The richest and most true gift of life, you previously took for granted or completely ignored in favor of alcohol will suddenly become extremely valuable to you.

The Evil Clown has spent decades of your life meticulously building a virtual reality. This matrix has been constructed around you so painfully slowly that you didn't even notice when it became complete. There are things and people in your life who you believe to be essential to your happiness and you are so convinced of this that you never question it.

Wake up call time! Most of your drinking buddies don't give a flying fuck about you. If you honestly believe all the people you hang out with to drink alcohol with on a regular basis are your friends, I have bad news for you.

Most drinkers look around at the regular faces of their fellow drinkers and see friends. Hell, after a few beers a few of them will be hugging you and telling you how much they 'fucking love you man'. This is like a fish in the middle of a large school of similar fish looking around and thinking 'wow I am so lucky, I have so many friends'.

Fish do not school because they are such great mates and they love each other. Fish group together as a survival instinct. This is purely an attempt to derive safety in numbers. A large school of fish from a distance looks like a big angry fish. This formation and pattern of behavior helps to protect from attack and nothing more.

Fish don't get together for fun or because they love chilling out as a gang. Guess what, drinkers do not hang out together because they love each other, even if they repeatedly state that's the reason. Drinkers school because it creates plausible deniability.

One individual sitting alone drinking neat vodka is a person in the depths of despair. Ten people sitting together drinking are a super fun group of sociable people. Even though they are all individually doing exactly the same thing as the lonely guy.

Drinking friends create a highly believable sense of safety in numbers. After all if you are drinking poison for fun and you can look around and get some instant social proof that what you are doing isn't insane, then happy days, right? Hey, Dave is a doctor, Jane is a lawyer and Mike is an architect – these are not stupid people and they drink, so how bad can it be right?

The Evil Clown doesn't care whether you drink alone or in a group. He knows there is no real safety in numbers but is very happy to let you to continue in that belief. Just so long as you keep drinking, he is happy for you to believe anything you want.

Sorry about this but when you stop drinking you are going to find out that a few of your friends are not as funny as you thought they were. You are going to discover that a lot of your 'friends' have nothing in common with you beyond a drug addiction. You will lose some friends when you stop drinking, that is the bad news. The good news is they were never your friends in the first place.

Do you really want to continue living inside a fake world with people pretending to be your friend?

Do you know what fake friends do when the shit hits the fan and you really need them? They disappear quicker than you can say 'hey I thought you said you loved me'.

Trust me on this, if you got ill and could never drink again, most of these amazing friends would delete you from their phone within days. You are only useful while you can validate their drug addiction as normal.

Nights spent drinking alcohol repeatedly are only fun if you are rendered stupid by the drug. You will find that living a sober life will force you to reassess what 'fun' means to you. This may be an uncomfortable adjustment but once you establish your new routine, you will be happier and more at peace than you ever thought possible.

How do I know? Because I have seen thousands of people go through this process and come out the other side.

Hold that thought… this morning one of my Stop Drinking Expert Facebook members posted something on this theme this morning:

Manic last week at work! Off to the beautiful island of Mallorca for 2 weeks in the sun on Monday and I can't wait!

Sober holidays are the best!

There is so much I am looking forward to, even the airport is a better experience sober, no stress or anxiety and impatience getting through check in and security because you can't wait for a drink! The whole experience is much more relaxing.

I have said this before but when drinking the only part of your day that matters is the bit while your drinking, the other bits are time spent feeling rough or counting down the minutes and hours, wishing them away until you can drink, when your sober and happy every part of the day becomes enjoyable, early mornings become fun and just as important as evenings it's like doubling your holiday time and it lasting twice as long!

Stop worrying about losing friends; it's a thinly veiled threat of the Clown and nothing more. If I could offer you the chance to buy some magic glasses that would instantly reveal who your real friends are and who are the ones who are only using you. Wouldn't you take me up on the offer? Of course and stopping drinking comes free with a pair of these amazing glasses.

Some people wonder if they can take some of their friends (or partner) on the sober journey with them. If they can just persuade their drinking friend to hold their hand and escape the trap side by side then they would have the best of both worlds. This is a particular hope and dream for many wives and husbands who have called time on alcohol and want their partner to come with them.

Sadly the path out of alcohol addiction isn't a path at all, it is a tightrope. There is not enough room on the wire to walk with someone by your side. Your drinking associate can walk ahead of you or they can follow you down the wire but it will always be a journey you take alone. You must be prepared to look back and find they have fallen off the wire and are no longer following you. There is nothing you can do about this, so don't waste too much time trying to control the uncontrollable.

The Evil Clown's Greatest Ever Trick

"My dear brothers, never forget, when you hear the progress of enlightenment vaunted, that the devil's best trick is to persuade you that he doesn't exist!", Charles Baudelaire

Perhaps the Evil Clown's greatest ever trick is persuading the Western world that it isn't a drug at all. Ask any regular wine drinker if they are a drug user and they will object in the strongest possible terms, they may even put their glass down first! Some of the most right thinking and level-headed people I know still insist that they drink to relax. However, if I visited their home one evening and in front of the children started sniffing glue, because I needed to relax, what do you think would happen?

They would demand I stop and if I refused I would be shown the door. What they are saying is; it is acceptable to use one drug to 'relax' but to use another is highly offensive. This illogical and flawed moral high ground comes from our social conditioning that alcohol is not a drug but rather a harmless social pleasantry. A luxury of life which can even be enjoyed liberally in the presence of impressionable children. And yet it is the very same harmless liquid that kills over 2,500,000 people every year. Even small countries' like the United Kingdom see nearly 400,000 people come to harm each year. What is worse, these are not static numbers – the problem is getting significantly worse over time.

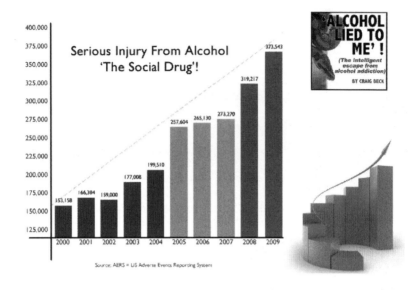

Serious Injury From Alcohol 'The Social Drug'!

153,158	166,384	159,000	177,008	199,510	257,604	265,130	273,270	319,217	373,543
2000	2001	2002	2003	2004	2005	2006	2007	2008	2009

Source: AERS = US Adverse Events Reporting System

How has the dark magician managed to hoodwink the Western world? The great relay race of drinking nearly always starts with your parents, and indeed their parents before them, and so on. When you are born into this world, you enter as a completely helpless, weak and fragile individual driven by the need for love. Strange looking giants surround you and over a space of time you notice that two of these giants appear to have taken an interest in you. They feed you, care for you and love you (despite your crying and constant demands on their time).

For many years, these two people are given the accreditation of being Gods in your eyes. It is completely inconceivable that they could ever be wrong or would ever lie or mislead you. Their words and actions are your gospel, and before the age of 5 you blindly accept information from this source without question. Everything you learn and witness at this tender age is stored permanently in your subconscious as a pure fact. In short, what you teach, show and expose your children to before the age of five will have a significant impact on how they turn out as adults.

Your experience with alcohol started from the moment you entered the world, it's more than likely the giants around you even used this poison to celebrate your arrival into the world. As you watched the giants popping corks out of attractive looking bottles, great smiles grew across their faces and laughter filled the room; what an amazing liquid this must be.

How strange that such a beautiful and unique gift is given to two happy people and they choose to herald the joyous arrival with a nice glass of a foul tasting depressant that removes our ability to consciously experience the wonderful things going on around us.

Alcohol is a tradition that has been passed down the family line from generation to generation (like a defective gene or biological bad penny). You only need to change the drug to see the truth behind the lies. If a bunch of friends came around to your house to meet your new baby and they all insisted on taking cocaine to wet the baby's head, I am sure you would have something to say.

I can make this point even clearer if you take a drug that has only recently become unacceptable. It's not so long back that a fine cigar was mandatory for the men folk to welcome in a new addition to the family. These days smoking over a newborn child would be seen as the height of irresponsibility. Alcohol is no different; it is a drug and nothing more.

Hang on a minute, you exclaim (as you continue to fight against the truth you already know), surely that's not a fair comparison. Smoking over a new born is bad because of the passive smoke you are enforcing the baby to inhale. It's not possible to passively drink. This is correct in physical terms but remember, everything you see at this impressionable age is a fact. From the child's point of view, why would one of the loving giants do something that is dangerous or wrong? Essentially, if their God drinks and it makes them happy, it must be something wonderful. Over the space of a few years the child will witness many thousands of occasions where pleasure is linked to alcohol. Birthday parties, Christmas, Mothers Day, Valentines Day and even family BBQ's. Repetition is the mother of all learning.

It's the same reason why it's unthinkable to consider throwing a party without having alcoholic drinks. You do it because it's always been done, but if your parents had not passed the poison chalice onto you, and you don't pass it onto your children, the tradition becomes diluted and eventually ineffectual. We don't have to conduct an extravagant experiment over several generations to prove this point. You only need to look at other cultures; Hinduism has many festivals and celebrations that are full of merriment, singing and dancing without a single drop of alcohol passing anyone's lips.

Alcohol does not make a party – people do! But just try throwing a party in your part of the world without any alcohol and half your guests will leave and go to the nearest pub. It's not that drinking creates fun, it's more that people who are out of control of their drinking are miserable without alcohol and can't think about anything else when they are without it. This isn't the fault of your party, it's the fault of society that teaches every one of us how to get addicted to a powerful and deceptive drug, and then compounds the problem by making us believe that it's normal.

Most people who drink wine everyday claim they honestly like the taste of it. This is nonsense; alcohol tastes so bad that the drinks manufacturers essentially have to find increasingly potent ways to cover it up. The body is an amazing and sophisticated piece of natural engineering. Despite what lies you have taught yourself on a superficial level, you still cannot break the rules your body has created over millions of years of evolution. Right at the top of our hierarchy of needs is the need to protect life, to stay alive at all costs. This is hardwired into every cell, every molecule and every tiny atom of your being. You can't decide to stop your heart beating or never to breathe again. You can't because it breaks the ultimate built-in rule; that of ensuring self-preservation at all costs.

The reason pure alcohol tastes bad is the same reason rotting meat or moldy, fungus infested bread tastes bad. Your body is warning you that you are consuming something that is putting you at risk. Think about it, in a hospital operating theatre, the room and the entire medical team that works in it must be 100% free of germs, bacteria and viral contaminants. So what do they scrub their hands with; not soap but alcohol. Because instantly on contact with any living organisms, it kills them dead! It pulls every bit of moisture out of their cells and causes them to implode in on themselves. At a micro cellular level, alcohol is a kin to thermo nuclear war; nothing survives. Do you honestly believe you have some amazing internal system to get around this fact? Somehow, when you consume this dangerous disinfectant it doesn't do the same level of damage because you have hidden it in a bit of cranberry juice.

Alcohol tastes horrible, you already know this but have forgotten, or as is more accurate, you have conditioned yourself to believe the opposite. As a hypnotherapist I can tell you that this is entirely possible and can be easily replicated in a relatively short space of time to prove the point. In hypnosis, the conscious (or thinking and judging) mind is bypassed, which means I can speak directly to the subconscious and implant beliefs without interference from the ego. Obviously, in therapy (and what you will find on the hypnosis tracks that accompany this book – available in the members area) all suggestions are positive and delivered for your benefit, but it is entirely possible for me to condition you to enjoy something deeply unpleasant, such as a hard punch on the arm! If while under hypnosis I hit you hard but told you it felt amazing and repeated that process many times and over several sessions, you would eventually begin to crave the experience.

You can see this feature of the human mind demonstrated in the most horrendous situations. When people are held captive by a sole individual and despite the fact that this person has abducted them, tortured and abused them, the victim slowly over time begins to develop feelings for the perpetrator. Despite suffering at the hands of this person, they become conditioned to their environment and begin to want to please the person who holds them against their will. This phenomenon has been studied at length by eminent psychologists and is known as 'Stockholm syndrome'.

To a certain degree I believe you are suffering from a form of this syndrome, alcohol has abused you for so long that you now firmly believe there is a benefit to you. You have fallen in love with a killer!

I say again, Alcohol tastes bad, your first interaction with it proved that point. When you first sneaked a drink of your father's neat whiskey, did it taste amazing? Or did it taste vile? Most people will say it tasted disgusting and they couldn't ever imagine getting hooked on something that tasted that bad. The taste of alcohol has not changed, so the only explanation for your current belief that it tastes good is that you have changed. You have conditioned yourself to believe booze tastes good. Don't feel bad; you have had a significant helping hand from society and the advertising industry.

What you must understand from this point on is that what you previously believed about booze was a lie and nothing more. If I poured a glass of pure alcohol and asked you to dip your little finger in and taste it, I am sure you will agree it would taste horrible, indeed, if you drank that glass of liquid you would shortly be dead. Funny really because since birth you have been programmed to ignore this and instead believe that alcohol is natural and an everyday part of life that you must consume if you are to be considered by your peers as a fun and social member of the gang. This is a throw back to our primitive evolution, we are still pack animals to a certain extent, and this is another reason for our global addiction to this drug.

The second reason is best explained by a smarter man than I, a famous psychologist called Abraham Maslow. Maslow is known for establishing the theory of a hierarchy of needs, writing that human beings are motivated by unsatisfied needs, and that certain lower needs need to be satisfied before higher needs can be.

Although there is a continuous cycle of human wars, murder, and deceit, he believed that violence is not what human nature is meant to be like. Violence and other evils occur when human needs are thwarted. In other words, people who are deprived of lower needs, such as safety, may defend themselves by violent means. He did not believe that humans are violent because they enjoy violence. Or that they lie, cheat, and steal because they enjoy doing it.

According to Maslow, there are general types of needs (physiological, safety, love, and esteem) and they must be satisfied before a person can act unselfishly. He called these needs "deficiency needs". As long as we are motivated to satisfy these cravings, we are moving towards growth, toward self-actualization.

Satisfying needs is healthy, and blocking gratification makes us sick and unhappy. In other words, we are all "needs junkies" with cravings that must be satisfied and should be satisfied. If we don't concentrate on doing this we will literally become sick. 'Will-power' is an illusionary weapon created by the egoic mind. It's like your enemy giving you a plastic sword and saying 'here, use this to protect yourself if I ever attack you!'

This is exactly why people have such a hard time trying to go cold turkey with their drinking. One morning you wake up and say, that's it I am never drinking again. By lunchtime you have a psychological itch so intense you are almost screaming inside.

Will-power does not work because it forces your subconscious and conscious mind into civil war. The exact same reason why the moment you go on a diet you become hungrier than you thought possible.

Here is the secret to stopping drinking; you need to attach more pleasure to not drinking than there is to drinking. You have to remove the need by understanding the truth about booze. It is not a social pleasantry but rather an attractively packaged poison. A multi billion dollar marketing campaign for the alcoholic drinks industry is working exceptionally hard to convince you otherwise, but you have to trust your gut on this one.

Let me put the point another way. I have two wonderful children who I love and adore more than life itself. Maybe you also have children yourself and you can understand my love and need to protect my children from the harms of the world? Let me ask you a question: If you had some strong rat poison for dealing with a tricky vermin infestation, would you keep it in a chocolate box and put it within reach of your kids?

Alcohol is similar to an anti-personnel landmine. You step on it and beyond a small clunk all appears fine… until you try and step off it. Then and only then you discover what a mess you are really in.

Our desire to drink is what we call a proponent need; this is a 'need' that has a powerful influence over our actions. Everyone has proponent needs, but those 'needs' will vary among individuals. A teenager may have a need to feel that he/she is accepted by a group. A heroin addict will need to satisfy his/her cravings for heroin to function normally in society, and because of the strength of the need they are unlikely to worry about acceptance by other people.

There is no difference between alcohol and heroin, or alcohol and nicotine. The only difference is alcohol is socially acceptable. But ask yourself this, if it had not yet been invented and I brought it to market tomorrow, do you think I would get it even half way through the rigorous testing process modern day food and beverages have to go through?

Around the world there is a very popular television programme called 'Dragon's Den', where would-be entrepreneurs pitch their ideas to already successful venture capitalists seeking investment. Can you imagine taking your fabulous new drink additive called alcohol before the Dragons and asking them to invest?

Entrepreneur: "Hello Dragons… I am here to ask for $1,000,000,000 to launch my new drink supplement called alcohol. Would you like to try a glass?"

A small sample of the product is poured into shot glasses for each of the investors in turn; cautiously they take a sip…

Dragons: "My God that tastes disgusting!"

Entrepreneur: "Yes, it does initially, but we have tested it quite extensively and find that people do eventually become accustomed to the taste. Plus, we use sweet tasting carrier beverages such as orange juice and cola to cover up the real taste. When they get used to it the consumer will feel amazing! Parties will go with a bang, everything seems funnier, and there is a massive euphoric sense of well being".

Dragons: "Sounds interesting, are there any down sides to this new drink?"

Entrepreneur: "Erm, well there is a slight risk of vomiting, sexually transmitted disease from unprotected sex, not to mention the violence and serious damage to careers, reputations and relationships. You probably need to be aware that several millions of our potential customers will have to die in agony from organ failure. Apart from that, I think this product has great potential".

Dragons: "I am not investing in that, I am out!"

Am I going to ridiculous extremes to make my point here? Perhaps, but no more ridiculous than people around the western world claiming that the disgusting liquid they took a sneaky drink of when their parents weren't looking as a kid. Has somehow turned into a gorgeous and moreish beverage that must be consumed. The booze tastes just as vile as it ever did, but you have allowed this attractively packaged poison to fit you with some very impressive rose-tinted glasses!

Here's an experiment for you, wait until Friday evening and go check your friends out of Facebook. You will see status after status along these lines:

"Wine O-Clock… I think so"

"Friday night and I can hear the beer monster calling'

"Friday night take away and a bottle of wine… it would be rude not to"

"Thank God it's the weekend, chilling out with a nice bottle of red"

"Enjoying a very large glass of wine… I love the weekends"

"Cheeky glass of wine on the go"

That last one particularly amuses me, to think that we could explain away what we are doing by adding a cute descriptive term before admitting the truth. You wouldn't hear this with any other drug would you? Imagine if we talked about heroin in the same way.

"Friday night, cheeky hit of heroin… it would be rude not to"

It's time to grow up and realize you have been scammed. Yes, you - the bright and worldly-wise individual who has a good job and a successful career. The very same person, who achieved all that, has been fooled by the oldest trick in the book.

You have become addicted to a drug, and this has created a recurring psychological itch that makes you want to scratch it at regular intervals. You have created a deficiency need, and according to Abraham Maslow, when the deficiency needs are met: Instantly other and higher needs emerge, and these, rather than physiological hungers, dominate the person. And when these in turn are satisfied, again new (and still higher) needs emerge, and so on. As one desire is satisfied, another pops up to take its place.

Maslow's next section of needs is those of love and belongingness. Humans have a desire to belong to groups: clubs, work groups, religious groups, family, gangs, etc. We need to feel loved by others, not so much in a sexual way; I suppose another way of putting it would be to say that we need to feel significant. We need to be accepted by others. Performers appreciate applause. We need to be needed. Beer commercials, in addition to playing on sex, also often show how beer makes for camaraderie. When was the last time you saw a beer commercial with someone drinking beer alone?

It doesn't matter how pretty the bottle, what the marketing claims or the sheer numbers of your friends who insist that alcohol is a harmless part of everyday social life. The devil is the devil and alcohol is a drug – whether you like it or not!

False Evidence Appearing Real

"Fear keeps us focused on the past or worried about the future. If we can acknowledge our fear, we can realize that right now we are okay. Right now, today, we are still alive, and our bodies are working marvelously. Our eyes can still see the beautiful sky. Our ears can still hear the voices of our loved ones",
Thich Nhat Hanh

The second most common explanation I hear from people to justify not taking action over their drinking is fear. The fear of taking a chance but not getting the desired result of happy sobriety.

I understand why drinkers feel like this. For the longest time we cling on to the belief that 'we can stop anytime we want to'. To try to stop and to fail robs us of this supportive belief. It's all just a part of the denial process. We can't cope with the prospect that we are not in control of the drug any more and so we do nothing to avoid getting the confirmation.

This is a bit like not opening the credit card bill so you don't really owe the money. The excuses and reasons to avoid taking action are endless and all of them are baseless or if you prefer, false evidence appearing real. None of those excuses are a valid reason not to quit drinking poison for fun.

They are all just pieces of graffiti that are sprayed on the walls of your comfort zone. As we approach the edge of the zone we notice that there are lots of brightly colored and aggressive looking warning signs. They scream that there is danger and risk beyond this point and for your own safety you should go no further!

The mistake we all make is we focus on the warning signs and not on what lies beyond them. It is true that if you try to stop drinking and fail you are going to feel bad about yourself. Really, I understand why someone would see that a way to avoid this pain is to not attempt to quit in the first place.

However, you have to step outside of yourself and see the bigger picture here. Instead of thinking about how you will feel if things go south. Think about how your life will change if you nail this and kick this filthy drug out of your world. Get super clear about what that scene would look like. Imagine yourself as an 85 year old man or woman who lived the remained of his or her life free of the attractively packaged poison that caused so much pain and suffering in their early life.

Make that image big, bright and beautiful in your mind. Next imagine you are laying on your death bed at age 65. You never took any action over your drinking and carried on with the addiction for fear of failure. Alcohol stole all your money, destroyed your family and

234

eventually you got so ill you could no longer work and provide for the people you love. You are dying, a poor broken man or woman and all the people you love and care for are having to sit by and watch you die. All because you were afraid to fail. Well guess what, by backing away from the edges of your comfort zone you got the very outcome you were trying to avoid!

This mind-set does not just apply to alcohol addiction. I want this to be a tool to release you from the life limiting loops created by fear. When we use the word fear we normally apply it to situations where we wrongly or rightly predict that we are at risk of harm. For example standing on the edge of a tall building generates a sensation of fear and anxiety so we become acutely aware of what could happen if we act inappropriately in those situations.

We can be afraid before a job interview because we have become attached to an outcome and don't want to experience rejection followed by the loss of that outcome. However, fear isn't always this obvious or dramatic but it can still be hugely limiting in our life.

When people go on a diet they start out with good intentions and a desperate desire to improve the way they look and feel. An honourable pursuit, but why do nearly 95% of them not only end up putting back on all the weight they lost plus and additional few pounds for good measure? The answer is fear, at the start of the diet the pain of looking in the mirror or not being able to squeeze into their favorite denim any more creates low level fear. For example 'what if I just keep getting bigger', 'what if I have nothing to wear at the party', 'what if they start calling me names at school' etc. So, we start the diet motivated to move our chubby body away from the fear. Then we lose a bit of weight and the original fear subsides but it is often replaced by a new concern. You see, we enjoy our tasty treats and takeaways in front of a good movie. Suddenly we feel like we are depriving ourselves of some of the fun bits of life. We fear that if we carry on being strict with ourselves we are going to be short changed by life and have less fun. Thus begins the yo-yo diet routine that dominates the life of so many.

I am writing this section of the book in the business class cabin of a British Airways flight from London Heathrow to Austin, Texas and even here fear is present. I am not talking about worrying about the plane crashing or running into some scary turbulence. I have been on board for just two hours and so far I have been offered free alcohol at least half a dozen times. I can't drink alcohol because it has a nasty habit of trying to kill me.

If you have read my book *Alcohol Lied to Me* you will know that I had a near two decade long battle with the booze and I became teetotal about six or seven years ago. I don't have to struggle to stay away from drinking, no part of me wants to go back where I was but there is an element of fear at the back of my head every time the airhostess comes down the aisle with the drinks trolley and I turn down a very expensive French Bordeaux and instead ask for a cheap glass of water. The northerner in me feels like I am getting ripped off – I feel like I am getting much poorer value for money than the guy next to me who has so far knocked back $100 worth of wine and brandy. I am 99% certain that I won't buckle in the name of value but I am acutely aware and afraid of that 1% that still lingers at the back of my mind.

Fear is present on a daily basis and in a myriad of ways. We are taught to be careful, to listen to fear and respond accordingly and the vast majority of society obeys this unwritten law. The result is a safer, more boring & less fulfilling life. This is the world of the Average Joe and the Average Jane – safe and steady but beige. What I am encouraging you to do is respond to fear in a highly counter intuitive way. Instead of seeing fear as a warning I want you to see it as an opportunity light blinking on the dashboard of your life. Essentially, if you are afraid of it then you must do it!

Fear Response Examples

Situation	Average Joe Response	Fearless Response
Afraid of drinking alcohol.	Path of least resistance. Surely just one won't hurt will	Take the least easy path. See it as a clear sign that

	it?	drinking won't serve you.
Afraid to approach the hot girl.	Don't do anything – let her walk out of his life.	Approach without a second thought. See the fear as a green light.
Afraid to go through with the charity parachute jump.	Cancel for 'health reasons' explains to friends they would love to but the doctor said no.	Fear means there is no other option but to do the jump. Everything else will make their comfort zone contract.

I can't begin to tell you how many people I meet who are full of regret, and virtually never about the things they have done in their life but much more commonly about the things they never did. The last time I saw my aunty Angela she was having a coffee with my parents at their home in Darlington. I joined them all for a short while and as I sat down Angela was expressing her regret that she had never learned to drive.

She had started to learn but got too afraid to ever put in for the test and it just became one of those things we label shoulda, woulda, coulda. Two years previously Angela had sadly been diagnosed with C.U.P. cancer

(cancer of unknown primary origin). She was still her old lively self but her prognosis was not great, all treatment had ultimately failed. The doctors estimated she had between six and nine months to live. Angela decided that before it became impossible she was going to take and pass her driving test.

She never got the chance as she died three weeks later. The moment she died passing or failing that driving test became irrelevant; all the fear about taking the test in the first place also became equally as irrelevant. There are dozens of things that you want in life that you don't have because fear is preventing you going after them.

One day in the future all that fear will be rendered pointless by the same event that Angela went through, the event that nobody has ever managed to avoid. What I am saying is that your ego is trying to protect you from harm by encouraging you to avoid risk by using fear as a virtual 10x4 to hit you about the head with.

Your body is like an apartment shared between two tenants. The ego and the soul, or if you prefer the conscious mind and the unconscious mind are the tenants of your body. The soul is eternal and divine, it is essentially a fragment of God and it knows this for certain. It is also acutely aware that the apartment it is renting is temporary and when the lease ends it will just move to a new place and start over.

However, the ego knows that when the lease ends that's the end of the story, its game over. This creates a sensation of blind panic for the ego, which point blank refuses to accept the situation. It kicks and screams trying to prove that it can prevent the lease from ending. Hey perhaps if you fill the apartment with more and more stuff and never leave so they can't come in and dump your possessions then perhaps the lease will continue evermore right? The ego is so terrified of the end it has been rendered insane by the constant thought of it.

Out of this insanity we get all the self-limiting beliefs that hold us back.

- Save for a rainy day
- What can go wrong, will go wrong
- What if I can't ever stop drinking
- I am not ready for my driving test
- I am not good enough for that promotion at work
- My life won't be worth living without a drink

The ego uses the past as a reverse projector in an attempt to control the uncontrollable. Fear is liberally applied to all areas of your life in the hope that it will keep you safe if completely unfulfilled. You are alive but miserable, that's good enough. The ego doesn't particularly care how happy you are, its primary focus is trying in vain to avoid the inevitable final act, at whatever cost.

What I am about to ask you to do is acknowledge that one of your tenants is insane and while you can't evict you can decide to stop listening to his/her insane ramblings. From this point on fear should be seen as the screams in the night of your troublesome tenant. All the predictions of doom, gloom, terror and trauma are nothing more than a desperate illusion.

Start living in the knowledge that the only moment that exists is this one, right here and right now. The past and the future do not exist and they never will – this is it and this is all there will ever be.

There is a percentage chance that this nineteen year old Boeing 777-200 aircraft will crash before I reach Austin, Texas – should I just stop writing now just in case? No of course not, because right here in this moment I am alive and as long as that situation continues I have a message to get out there.

Exercise:

I want you to stop reading at this point and take a little life inventory. Grab a pen and paper and write down everything you can think of that you have wanted to achieve but have been prevented doing so by fear. Perhaps you have always wanted to skydive but can't quite bring yourself to sign up for a jump. Maybe there is a senior position opening at work and you have told yourself that you are not quite ready and maybe try again in a few years. Perhaps you have been head over heals in love with Nicola on reception for years and never done anything about it?

On a blank piece of paper draw four columns, in the first column write your goal, in the second write down how fear is preventing you from achieving this goal, in the third column write down what will happen if you continue to let fear dominate this area of your life and in the final column I want you to imagine how you would feel if you ignored the 'Danger Do Not Pass' signs hanging on the wall of your comfort zone and charged on through regardless.

Example:

Goal	Fear	Failure	Success
To skydive	I might die, or worse I might embarrass myself by refusing to jump!	It will always be there as something that says 'you are a coward'.	I will feel invincible. I will have done something most people would never be brave enough to do. I would feel huge pride in myself.

One of the most positive motivational speakers that America ever produced was Zig Ziglar. He would describe the start of his day in such a beautiful way. He used to say 'every morning at 6am my opportunity clock would go off and wake me up. I don't call it an alarm clock because that's negative. That bell signals the start of a whole new day full of wonderful opportunities'.

As ever I want this to be a practical investment of your time and money, something that you can take and implement quickly into your life and consequently see massive positive change as a result. I am going to close this penultimate chapter on fear with a challenge, for you to do one thing right now that fear has been making you avoid. It could be something as simple as picking up the phone and apologizing to someone you didn't act in the right way with. It could be clicking send on a resignation email or a job application form – find something that you are afraid of and embrace it as an opportunity.

"I think that the power is the principle. The principle of moving forward, as though you have the confidence to move forward, eventually gives you confidence when you look back and see what you've done." – Robert Downey Jr.

I am assuming you came to this book with a desire to stop drinking but were not quite sure how to go about it. I am hoping by now that desire has intensified, you now see booze for what it really is, and you are determined never to drink that foul tasting, life destroying poison that is alcohol again. If you are still hoping to go back to drinking one day, or are planning just to cut down, let me explain why that is a very bad idea.

All addictive drugs have what is known as a kick, the period after you stop taking them in which the side effects occur. Luckily for you, we are talking about an alcohol kick here, which is relatively mild compared to other street drugs. The reason heroin is so difficult to get off is because the kick is so intense and painful that the user has to endure agony knowing that all the pain could be made to vanish in a split second by just taking another hit of the drug.

Alcohol withdrawal begins from the moment you take your last sip, and will reach its peak intensity between 24 and 48 hours later. This is why many people become evening drinkers, and the first thing they do when they get home after a hard day at work is reach for the bottle opener. As they arrive home they are exactly mid-way through the most powerful phase of the withdrawal process. Alcohol withdrawal is so subtle that we are unable to identify the symptoms unless we are aware of what to look for. Withdrawal from booze feels like a general feeling of unease, to the everyday person it may feel a little like stress or anxiety. This is why people incorrectly claim that a drink when they get home from work helps them unwind. The only thing that first drink does is turn off the withdrawal symptoms of

246

the previous days drinking. So to a certain extent it's true; they do feel instantly less stressed, because the general unease and anxiety directly created by the alcohol has now gone, but if they hadn't drank the day before, it wouldn't have been there in the first place. So all you are fixing is the previous day's mistake.

The full chemical withdrawal from alcohol, regardless of the amount you drink, lasts around two weeks, climbing to a climax around 36 hours after the last drink and slowly fading away to near zero after a couple of weeks. Because of the hard wiring you have constructed in your brain, and your overactive hypothalamus, you may never achieve total zero, but everyday you don't drink, the base state of withdrawal drops a little further.

If you are currently dependent upon alcohol to the point where if you stop you experience traumatic physical symptoms such as spasms, fitting, fever and vomiting, you will need to see your doctor and explain that you are using this method to stop. Your general practitioner will be able to give you prescription medication to help suppress these unpleasant side effects while you go through the kick.

This extended withdrawal period is exactly why you cannot safely have 'just one drink', that one drink is the reason why 95% of people trying to quit with 'will-power' fail. One sip of alcohol may take less than five seconds to consume, but will start an unstoppable process that will last at least two weeks. During that period a new chemical imbalance will force you to crave another drink and that pain will only stop for two reasons. Firstly, the discomfort will go away if you take a drink of alcohol, and secondly, that pain will dissipate if you give it long enough. So in summary, the only way to stop the pain of an alcohol kick is to drink or to not drink. Only one of those solutions doesn't create another problem the next day, and I don't need to tell you which one.

If for the briefest moment you start to think 'just one drink won't do any harm' or 'I will only have one glass of wine with my evening meal', you are willingly stepping back into the mousetrap and assuming that this time you are safe, one more poke at the cheese won't make any difference!

You drink because there is a chemical imbalance in your brain, but the catch 22 is that while the alcohol gives you a short-term release from the imbalance by flooding the brain with more of the chemicals you crave. Withdrawal from alcohol also causes a chemical imbalance all of its own. So now you have two problems; one created by the booze, and one that was there in the first place. The discomfort of the first imbalance makes you create the second imbalance and you get trapped in a never-ending loop.

Whenever we try to correct something about ourselves that we don't like we nearly always reach for willpower as our first choice of weapon. This self-defeating choice is similar to bringing a spoon to move a mountain. As I explain in my book 'Alcohol Lied to Me', willpower is completely ineffective against hard-wired subconscious problems. It is this reason my 95% of diets fail and why Alcoholics Anonymous has a success rate under 7%. AA and the big book theory of alcohol addiction insist that problem drinkers are forever to struggle against the temptation to drink. They will never be cured and will always be labeled as recovering alcoholics.

If your purchase of this book was precipitated by worry about your own drinking then I am almost certain that you have already tried to significantly cut down or stop completely already. Of course you failed but then you never had anything more than a 5% chance of success in the first place. The reason for this is your brain is independently intelligent; it completes tasks whether you consciously ask it to or not. Thankfully you don't have to remember to breathe or beat your heart. When you repeatedly do something the brain knows that consciously thinking through the task is a resource heavy and highly ineffective way to get the job done. Conscious (willpower) processing is fine for one off tasks but for regular activities it is illogical, and so the brain uses protein and amino acids to build physical pathways to automatically complete the job in the future. Essentially you have a self-made computer chip in your mind that beats your heart, another to control your body temperature and now one to facilitate your drinking habit.

For your own protection you are prevented from consciously accessing these chips. It might seem strange that you can't control a part of your own earthly body. But imagine if you had the ability to lift the hood and tinker with the machinery that controls how you process oxygen, how you walk and sleep. I struggle jump-starting an automobile never mind messing with a machine as complex and powerful as the human brain.

I stopped drinking alcohol by coming up with a method to remove these erroneous programs running in the subconscious mind. It is the same technique that thousands of others have replicated to cure their own drinking problems via my books and online stop drinking club.

The principles of my stop drinking method are:

1. Dissecting the current behavior
2. Understanding the reality
3. Dealing with the kick
4. Correcting the chemical imbalance via supplementation
5. Subconscious reprogramming

The whole process starts with what you do next. Nothing happens until something moves, as the saying goes. That something has to be you, nobody else is going to do this for you. I want to close this book by giving you very clear steps to take next.

1. Watch The Movie 'Click'

The objective of this book is not just for you to stop drinking, but also for you to find that your new sober lifestyle delivers with it real happiness. There is no point being sober and miserable. So many people spend their lives ignoring (or drowning out with alcohol) internal alarm bells ringing all over the place. Something inside is trying to tell these people that something vital to their peace and happiness is

252

missing. But rather than deal with this internal void they throw a rug over the hole inside them and pretend it isn't there. Alcohol hides the problem but it doesn't fix it.

2. Catch the Evil Clown at work

Become conscious of the Evil Clown trying to hijack your thinking. All statements that begin with the word 'I' are a clear indication that the ego is speaking.

For example

- I deserve a drink.
- I can have one drink as a treat.
- I can control my drinking this time.
- I had a hard day, I need a drink to relax.

You will also notice that all these statements come from a position of fear. The word 'deserve' implies that you have suffered and this should be recognised with a reward. The word 'have' suggests that you believe you need an external substance to make you happy and the word 'control' is easily identified as a negative element. The Clown speaks from a position of fear. However, the real you (which knows exactly what you need to be healthy and happy) always speaks from a position of love, always!

This is the voice you should be listening to.

3. Find your purpose

Many people are using alcohol to cover up a feeling of emptiness within them. If you are not happy with the direction of your life, the quicker you make a course correction the quicker things will start to improve. Alcohol is trapping you on a path that ultimately won't serve you. That nagging voice inside you is there to remind you that you are here for a profound and important reason. That something inside you is trying to motivate you to take action. In the past you have dealt with this nagging sensation by drinking alcohol (a mild anaesthetic) to try and make it go away.

I don't know what it is for you, but there is almost certainly something you enjoy doing so much that when you do it time flies by. Whether this is painting, photography, running your own business or just playing golf – find the thing you are passionate about and do it... a lot! I am also certain that at the moment alcohol is stealing enough of your time to prevent you pursuing this passion of yours.

4. Kick the kick

Be prepared for alcohol to kick and scream like a petulant child when you try to quit. For up to two weeks you may experience mild sensations of anxiety and or stress. These are nothing more than cravings being generated by the drug to try and force you back to the bottle. Remember, the reason why alcohol has the power to kill 3.5 million people every year is its ability to trick otherwise intelligent individuals into consuming attractively packaged poison. Ask yourself what do alcohol dependant people do when they are stressed out? Yes, that's right they drink. The Alcohol Monster knows this and so it will try and induce stress and anxiety in you with the goal of getting you to respond in your usual and predictable way. You may come home from work having had the bitch of all days and believe that you deserve a drink more than anything else. Despite how powerfully and logical it appears, remember what it really is and don't fall for it!

Make sure you have understood the tapping techniques and other craving control strategies we talked about in chapter six. The chemical kick from alcohol is gone after two weeks; things get much easier from this point.

5. Don't lie down with dogs

You are making an important lifestyle decision. This choice is a lot easier if you surround yourself with people who support and encourage you. If you tell your drinking friends that you are thinking of quitting booze they will in all likelihood attempt to sabotage your efforts.

This might sound like strange behaviour to expect from people who are supposed to love and care for you.

However, what you must remember is alcoholism is a learned addiction. We all had to work very hard over many years to teach ourselves to ignore the horrible taste, painful hangovers and in built knowledge that we are knowingly consuming poison for fun. All drinkers carry a nagging worry that what they are doing must one day stop, but most people respond to this by sticking their fingers in their ears to block out this painful truth.

So, when you quit drinking and come across all *goody two shoes the teetotaller* you subconsciously cause them pain. All human beings will respond to pain by trying to either move away from it or make it stop. Your friends and family are unlikely to disown you because you stopped drinking but whether they are conscious of it or not they may try to tempt you back into the alcohol fold, so that you are no longer causing them pain. Watch out for innocent statements such as 'surely you can have one drink' or 'come on don't be anti social, just have one'. I don't believe there is any maliciousness in this behaviour, most people are not even aware they are doing it. It is simply a truth that people prefer to take the path of least resistance and that means it is easier to persuade you to lower your standards rather than attempt to raise their own.

Expecting support from other drinkers in your pursuit of giving up alcohol is fruitless. Essentially if you lie down with dogs you will get up with fleas. I strongly advise you to try and be around people who share your goal or at least agree with your decision. Perhaps you have a few friends who also want to stop drinking, why not get together and support each other? However, if you are making this journey alone, you can find local support groups such as AA or even join my private Facebook page. The members of this hidden club are truly amazing people. I constantly amazed at just how much they reach out to help and encourage each other and share beautiful stories of how their lives have turned around since they stopped drinking. Membership is free, you can get more information from my website.

6. Take 100% responsibility

The world you experience might be the same as the world I experience but it is equally as possible that it is entirely unique to you. How do we know that when we both look at the color blue that it appears the same to both of us?

This is your own personal universe; it's time to take responsibility for your creation and stop pointing the finger of blame and making excuses. How often have you decided to go on a diet but at the last minute opted to start on Monday rather than straight away. How often have you delayed taking action on your drinking until after summer, after Christmas, after the dog's birthday? Make a commitment that you will break that loop today.

Imagine you are floating on your back in a river, gently flowing with the water. Suddenly the water begins to start flowing faster and faster and you find yourself going over a waterfall. Having splashed awkwardly over the edge and recovered your composure you probably wouldn't start blaming the waterfall for what happened, you would not take it personally. But this is what we do with life, shit happens and our ego insists that it's personal. Most of the time it isn't and blame never solves anything.

The ego likes to stick labels on things:

- The new car in your drive = good thing
- The tax demand in your mail box = bad thing
- The vacation you have planned = good thing
- Your boss won't give you time off work = bad thing

Labels are actions of the ego and always come from a position of fear. They distract you from taking responsibility and encourage you to point the finger of blame. Most labels are an illusion because they are highly subjective. For example if you found $50 in the street you would probably label that event a good thing but it certainly wasn't for the person who lost it. They would label it a bad thing, the same event becomes both good and bad at the same time – so what is the point of a label. It is neither good nor bad, it just is!

So you have a drink problem, you can blame your stressful job, your genetics or even something as vague as 'your crappy luck' but it won't help you stop drinking. Accept responsibility for the problem you have, there is no need or point in labelling yourself as weak willed or any other negative description. Your alcohol problem is a waterfall in your river of life, it happened – so deal with it and move on.

7. Reprogram your subconscious

The final step in the 'Escaping The Evil Clown' is subconscious reprogramming. As we have discussed, all the issues we face in life are our responsibility, as they are manifested directly by us, via the programs that run in our subconscious mind. Most of these sub-routines are beneficial and serve a valuable purpose such as controlling our body temperature and keeping us breathing at the correct rate.

However, along our journey through this life we pick up the odd erroneous program that creates unhelpful manifestations. These 'bad programs' make us fat, create low self-esteem and even get us addicted to harmful substances.

Thankfully we are prevented by nature from lifting the hood on the subconscious mind and tinkering with the engine. Of course our ego would have us believe that we are master mechanics, fully capable of making perfect adjustments to this most powerful of computers.

The subconscious knows better and the gate is kept firmly closed to the over zealous ego.

Using hypnosis we can bypass the conscious mind and implant positive corrections directly into the subconscious. As this part of the mind has no ability to judge or question, the implanted commands are run exactly as requested.

This section of the method is optional and many have stopped drinking completely without ever having used one of my hypnosis downloads. However, as with everything else I have told you so far. This was an important element for me and I want you to use every tool in the box to ensure we get the job done in one painless motion. If you do think these powerful audio tracks would help you then please stop by my website for the mp3 download details.

It is important that we ensure we fully understand what hypnosis is, or more importantly what it is not. Hypnosis is not black magic, a party trick nor a piece of theatre. It is a naturally occurring process of the brain that has unfortunately attracted some seriously bad press over recent years; some might say even OJ Simpson has had better press than hypnosis!

Thankfully, for over two thousand years it was documented and practiced with a great deal of respect. How bizarre that this long studied and amazing action of the human mind was essentially defamed by a man in a bar trying to convince girls to remove their clothes.

The traditional stage hypnotist is considered by most right thinking hypnotherapists and psychologists as a blundering incompetent dabbling in something they don't truly understand. If they did understand the amazing process they are playing with, I would suggest they would find something more productive to do with it than make a person believe they are a little fluffy duck called Roger!

A common misconception about hypnosis is that it is sleep. Although a hypnotized person appears to be sleeping, they are actually quite alert. Hypnosis is very difficult to describe, as nobody actually knows what is going on inside the mind of a subject. What we do know is that while in the trance state, the subject becomes very suggestible. A subject's attention, while they are going into trance, is narrowed down gradually.

Many areas of normal communication are removed one by one. Starting with sight, a person is asked to close his eyes and concentrate. Other senses are then removed from the equation; some people even lose complete feeling of their body. That may sound frightening, but it is accomplished in a slow, pleasant way, rather than suddenly turning off of a switch.

You enter a world of hyper relaxation and at the same time hyper awareness. As you might expect, as you remove certain senses the remaining ones become more acute to compensate. Often people who have been under hypnosis will come around and claim, "it did not work". When you enquire as to why they believe hypnosis did not occur, they make statements such as "I could hear everything", "I could even hear the cars going past the window!" This is all part of the misconception that hypnosis is sleep, and that during trance you are unconscious, when in actual fact you are hyper conscious.

I am telling you about hypnosis not because I want you to take to the stage, but because I want you to understand the truly amazing power of the subconscious mind. A person in hypnosis is highly suggestible. The hypnotist has direct access to the person's subconscious without having to go through the conscious mind. This is how they can convince a six-foot tall, 250lb man he is a light gentle ballet dancer and have him pirouetting his way around the stage.

Hypnosis is so natural, that you do it dozens of times a day without even realizing it. Have you ever driven home at the end of your working day and arrived home with no memory of the journey? Hypnosis just paid you a visit, your brain was using the opportunity of this familiar and fairly simple task to filter and file information in your brain.

You may notice yourself at work blankly staring at the computer screen in a deep peaceful daydream. This happens due to the vast amount of information constantly entering your brain, every few hours your mind must pause a little to filter and file all the information you have learned. Placing it in the correct storage area of the brain.

For example, let's say in the last hour your brain has learned that the color of the walls in the canteen are yellow. It has also learnt that your new managers' name is David. It must ensure the information you will need on an ongoing basis is stored close to hand. Unfortunately this is at the expense of the canteen walls, and I am sorry to say, if questioned, you may have trouble remembering what color those walls were - but who cares, walls may have ears, but I have noticed they stay pretty dumb when asked for a pay rise!

In my online stop drinking club, I use hypnosis to further embed the six steps of my stop drinking method. I do this because I know that the conscious mind is a guard dog. The sort of animal the mail man must first distract before he opens the gate and creeps up the path to post the mail through the letterbox, after doing so he sneaks back out, hopefully without being noticed.

During this book I have been directly talking to your guard dog, you can choose to accept what I am saying, or dismiss it. During hypnosis you do not have that problem; all suggestions are accepted without judgment because the words are directed to the subconscious.

Don't lie there waiting for something magical to happen, don't expect or demand anything, you will also need to be prepared to catch your ego trying to pull you out of the moment. It's fine when it does, if you find your mind wandering just notice what has happened, smile and refocus on the now. Relax and let the music and my words drift over you. There is nothing that you can do wrong, free yourself of that concern and let go of all expectation.

Part of the fear of giving up drinking is that you might spend the rest of your life with an itch you can't scratch; Living in a permanent state of wanting a drink but not being able to touch it. This is not a cure; this is a torturous and constant battle with the ego that you can't possibly expect to win in the long term. Imagine being so at ease with alcohol that you can honestly say you don't want a drink, you don't like the taste of it, and if someone pushed a glass of it into your hand you would rather go out of your way to find a replacement than take the slightest sip. This state is possible, I know because I have been through the process I have just described to you, and now I live it everyday.

Thank you for reading Escaping The Evil Clown with me, I sincerely hope it helps you take the first step out of this very destructive loop of alcohol addiction. When you get to the point where you can confidently claim that alcohol is no longer a part of your life I want to hear from you. Please contact me via the website and let me know just how many amazing things have appeared in your life since you got rid of the attractively packaged poison.

Remember, if you need a little extra help with this process then you can join my VIP mentoring program at www.StopDrinkingExpert.com

If you have enjoyed this book please would you go back to the online store where you bought it and leave a rating and review? This little act will take but a few minutes and it will really help get this valuable material to more people who desperately need it.

Recommended links

- http://www.CraigBeck.com
- http://www.StopDrinkingExpert.com

Follow Craig Beck on Social Media

- Facebook:

  https://www.facebook.com/craigbeckbooks

- Twitter: http://twitter.com/CraigBeck

You Don't Have to Do It Alone…

Join the online coaching club that has helped over 50,000 people just like you to get back in control of their drinking.

Download the total control alcohol course as soon as you join

Why not decide now and start to feel the benefits within 24 hours of joining

7 Life changing aspects to joining today

1. Significantly more effective than cold turkey or willpower methods.

2. 100% private & confidential solution – completely online process.

3. Protects your career – no need to take time off work to attend therapy.

4. Personal support from best selling author and ex-drinker Craig Beck.

5. No prescription drugs – no medication with problematic side effects.

6. Save thousands – the average Stop Drinking Expert member saves over $3000 per year.

7. Repair relationships – become a better parent, partner and friend.

I have been where you are...

Why you should believe me on this?... I am not a doctor telling you to drink less. I know it's not that easy!

My program works so well because I have been in the same alcohol-trap as you and escaped... Two bottles of wine a night and even more at the weekends was normal for me.

I know you don't want to stand up and call yourself an alcoholic. Actually I don't believe you are, as soon as you get started I will tell you exactly why this is the case.

100% private solution

I understand you don't want to risk your career or have any sign of this problem on your medical records. With my online stop drinking cure, you can deal with this in 100% privacy.

Another of the things you are going to love about my control alcohol system is you will be able to cut down or even how to quit drinking completely

When you get started today and join the thousands of other who are back in control of their drinking.

269

Made in the USA
Columbia, SC
29 August 2018